Praise for *Meditation*

"Encyclopedic in scope, this useful compendium is not just for newcomers on the spiritual path. Author Patrick Harbula covers every aspect of meditation from its history to its benefits to the how-tos of more than two dozen practices. A lifetime of experience with Eastern and Western contemplative traditions informs these pages, packed with useful tips on choosing a method, what to expect, and establishing a daily practice. Meditation fundamentals like breathwork, mindfulness, and visualization are explained in clear, accessible terms."

—Joan Duncan Oliver, author of *Buddhism: An Introduction to the Buddha's Life, Teachings, and Practice*

"Meditation is a very simple process which can be done in many ways. Patrick Harbula provides a guide that can be read as a basic primer or as a deep dive into all things meditation. This is a book that should be on every meditator's bookshelf and be dog-eared, marked up, and well-read."

—Dr. Jim Lockard, author of *Creating the Beloved Community: A Handbook for Spiritual Leadership*

"In *Meditation* Patrick Harbula offers perhaps the most inclusive explanation and application of meditation I have ever read. He has taken what is generally perceived as an Eastern practice and made it user-friendly for the Western mind. This is an exquisite and transparent handbook for anyone who seeks to explore the countless benefits found in a life grounded in meditation. I encourage you to allow Patrick to be your personal guide on the journey to the place you never really left—your oneness with Life. He knows—in real time—from whence he speaks."

—Dr. Dennis Merritt Jones, bestselling author of *The Art of Abundance: Ten Rules for a Prosperous Life* and *The Art of Uncertainty: How to Live in the Mystery of Life and Love It*

"Patrick Harbula's presentation of a wide variety of meditation styles and techniques makes this book a unique presentation on the subject. Particularly insightful is the Helpful Hints section, which offers practical and cutting-edge strategies for effortlessly stilling the mind. The chapter on Supportive Spiritual Practices also makes this book a seminal and complete treatment for spiritual growth as well as user-friendly tool for beginners and seasoned meditators alike."

—Dr. Ken Gordon, spiritual director of Centers for Spiritual Living

"Patrick Harbula has created a beautiful introduction to the novice meditator. Using gentle humor, personal stories, and practical suggestions, he guides the reader through complex ideas such as enlightenment, spiritual bypass, dealing with expectations, and sustaining an enjoyable and meaningful meditation practice."

—Dr. Edward Viljoen, author of *The Power of Meditation: An Ancient Technique to Access Your Inner Power*

"While explaining the deep, historical roots of meditation, Patrick makes the practice very accessible to the beginner and highly motivational for the longtime meditator. This is one of the most comprehensive books on meditation available to us today. Benefits, approaches, and specific practices are skillfully explained in his approachable personal style, and I recommend it wholeheartedly."

—Rev. Dr. Maxine Kaye, author of *Alive and Ageless: How to Feel Alive and Live Fully Every Day of Your Life*

Meditation

THE SIMPLE AND PRACTICAL WAY
TO BEGIN AND DEEPEN MEDITATION

Patrick J. Harbula D.D.

ROBINSON

ROBINSON

First published in the US in 2019 by St. Martin's Essentials,
an imprint of St. Martin's Publishing Group

First published in Great Britain in 2019 by Robinson

1 3 5 7 9 10 8 6 4 2

Important Note
This book is not intended as a substitute for medical advice or treatment.
Any person with a condition requiring medical attention should consult a qualified
medical practitioner or suitable therapist.

A CIP catalogue record for this book is available from the British Library.

ISBN: 978-1-47214-438-6

Printed and bound in Great Britain by Clays Ltd, Elcograf S.p.A.

Papers used by Robinson are from well-managed forests
and other responsible sources.

Robinson
An imprint of
Little, Brown Book Group
Carmelite House
50 Victoria Embankment
London EC4Y 0DZ

An Hachette UK Company
www.hachette.co.uk

www.littlebrown.co.uk

How To Books are published by Robinson, an imprint of Little, Brown Book Group.
We welcome proposals from authors who have first-hand experience of their subjects.
Please set out the aims of your book, its target market and its suggested contents in an
email to howto@littlebrown.co.uk.

This book is dedicated to my most influential teachers of meditation, including: Mark Beshara, Dr. Earl Barunum, Dr. Vivian King, Djual Khul from the Alice Baily teachings, Satya Sai Baba, Ram Das, Anandamayi Ma, and St. Teresa of Avila. And all those saints, sages, and explorers of the inner realms who have paved the way for the evolution of consciousness through meditation as well as all those seekers to come, including you, my beloved reader.

CONTENTS

ACKNOWLEDGMENTS

I want to express my deep appreciation for all those who have contributed to this book, including: Joel Fotinos, for inviting me to write it and all his encouragement throughout; Bethany Reis, for copyediting; Richard Oriolo, for page design; Tania Bissell, for proofreading; valuable feedback and input from friends Jeffrey Gero, Jenny Gago, Rev. Stephen Rambo, Rev. Maur Horton, Kim Robinson, and Gretchen Cassidy; Tracy Marcynzsyn, for the initial copyedit; and my lovely wife and partner, Corina Villeda, for help with research and feedback.

INTRODUCTION

Isn't it interesting reflecting back on certain events in life that led us in a particular direction? Perhaps we would end up in a similar place if we hadn't experienced the same events, or perhaps we wouldn't. My sense and belief is that we would arrive at a similar station and philosophy of life, but certainly not exactly the same. Nevertheless, the path that led me to a life of meditation unfolded in what seemed like random events, but I am certain I would have landed here one way or another.

My first job, at sixteen, working for someone other than my mom as her tennis instructor assistant, was stringing tennis rackets at Paramount Sports Tennis Shop in Hollywood. I made three dollars per racket. This was at a time when tennis was extremely popular in the United States. Lots of people were taking lessons and learning and playing the sport, so there were tennis shops in most cities in Southern California and Paramount Sports, which I always assumed was named such because of its proximity to Paramount Studios, was the most popular shop in Los Angeles County.

But how did this job lead me to a forty-two-year practice of meditation and ultimately writing this book? My boss at the time was not only an excellent businessman and shop owner, but also a mystic. He invited me to attend an introductory meeting at a training called Mind Probe One and told me if I wanted to take the weeklong training, he would pay for half, which I think left me with a price tag of 150 dollars. Upon attending an introductory meeting, I thought the process seemed pretty weird. On the other hand, weird was not much of a deterrent for me. In fact, it was more like an incentive. As an introspective and inquisitive child and throughout my life, I have consistently challenged traditional beliefs and societal norms.

There were many aspects of the training that I won't go into, but the primary process was a meditation technique called the Color Cycle—essentially imagining yourself surrounded and immersed in the colors of the spectrum and rainbow in succession—red, orange, yellow, green, blue, indigo, violet, and finally, white. Each color represents a specific energy and quality, and white represents the center of the mind, where all things are possible. There were many other techniques and practices involved in the training, including visualization, psychic diagnosis, and energy healing, but all of them were preceded by the Color Cycle process.

After completing the weeklong training, I continued to do the meditation practice for many years. The only classes I found of interest in late high school and college were philosophy, psychology, and a smidgeon of sociology, but I hadn't studied much Eastern philosophy up to that point. Purely as a result of meditation practice and not from the influence of any reading or teaching, at twenty years old, I had a mystical experience, where I knew and felt myself as one with the Infinite Universe. I was given answers to any and all questions. I knew without a doubt that everything and all sentient beings were part of one interconnected organism we can call the Infinite Universe, or God. Every action or occurrence affects the whole and everything and everyone within the whole. Time is an illusion. At the level of true reality, everything that has ever happened or ever will happen occurs at the same time, in one moment. I was going to write "the present moment," but there isn't even a present moment, because that would mean there is a past and a future.

It wasn't until I was twenty-three that I found New Thought philosophy, specifically Science of Mind (named after a book written by Ernest Holmes), which includes a strong influence of Eastern and Western metaphysics and an emphasis on meditation and affirmative prayer. I found in New Thought a community of people who understood (at least at a conceptual level for some and an experiential level for others) what I had already learned from my own mystical experience.

My journey was somewhat backward from that of most people on a meditative path who learn about metaphysics and spiritual philosophy, then start a practice, then (for those who take it to a deeper level) have mystical experiences. I had the mystical experience through my meditation practice, which ultimately led me to be part of a larger community of like-minded people and a student of many different meditation schools. My studies in this system led me to become ordained as a Minister of Spiritual Awareness in 1986 by the late Dr. Earl Barnum, a pioneer in the field of New Thought and Religious Science. I later affiliated with

Religious Science International in 2010, which is now called Centers for Spiritual Living.

While I am writing this book from a spiritual practice, it is important to emphasize that embarking on a spiritual path is not at all necessary to receive the benefits from meditative practice, but if you continue to meditate, don't be too surprised if you sooner or later deepen your appreciation for the inner realms of your own consciousness and the mystery of life.

At twenty-one, I followed in my mother's footsteps along the path of a tennis-teaching professional. I taught visualization techniques (a form of meditation I will write about later) to my tennis students to help them improve their performance on the court. I found that people who practiced these techniques in addition to physical practice would improve at a much faster rate than those who did not. Scientific studies corroborate my own findings. I also invented a practice called Zen Tennis, which I will elucidate in chapter 4, "Meditation Practice."

Many of my students reported that they used these techniques to improve other areas of their lives. Eventually, it occurred to me that this is really good stuff that needs to get out to larger numbers of people. At age twenty-seven, I was teaching a class called The Nature of the Soul, which had a strong emphasis on meditation practice and spiritual service and had a profound effect on my spiritual evolution. The entire class and one additional person became the first staff to produce *Meditation Magazine*, a national, full-color trade magazine that was published from 1985 to 1992.

During that period, I also completed a four-year training in psychosynthesis, a form of transpersonal psychology, with the High Point Foundation in Pasadena under the late Dr. Vivian King. This system was another powerful teaching that enhanced my spiritual and meditation journey. The main emphasis of the teaching is that we are more than our sensations, feelings, and thoughts. In fact, there is a meditation practice that asks us to observe these three elements of the personality and finally ask the question, "If I can observe my sensations, feelings, and thoughts, who is doing the observation? Who is the 'I' that can observe and choose how to express through my threefold personality?" Once I completed my training, I offered lectures and classes in spiritual psychology and continued to offer spiritual counseling and classes in other metaphysical subjects as well.

When I went into academic publishing at Sage Publications (a world-renowned social science publisher) in 1992, I offered "stress-reduction" sessions each morning for anyone in the company who wanted to attend. I also did visioning sessions with my staff (twenty-five in my first managerial position and seventy-five at the height of my director position). The production department that I managed became a model for efficiency in the corporation. We achieved unprecedented success, some of which was a result of wisely applied business strategies, but I'm certain that our levels of success would not have been fully realized without the application of strategic meditative practices.

All the experiences above inspired me to write my popular book, published in 2002, *The Magic of the Soul: Applying Spiritual Power to Daily Living*, which is a compilation of all the philosophies and spiritual practices that led me to a life of success and inner fulfillment. The book naturally includes a heavy emphasis on meditation and a chapter specifically on the subject. After its publication I left the corporate world and embarked on a career of traveling; speaking; offering workshops on various subjects, including meditation; and life and/or spiritual coaching, as well as training and certifying life coaches in what we call consciousness coaching.

I haven't quite thought of this realization in these terms until writing this paragraph, but my work as a life coach and coach trainer is primarily about assisting people to live in the state that is consistent with the consciousness that results from extended years of meditation—the consciousness of love, freedom, joy, creativity, and expanded insight.

People most often come to life or spiritual coaching because they want to achieve some goal, but what they realize through the Living Purpose Institute method of consciousness coaching is that the most important element in achieving one's goals is to *live from the energy of the completed vision.* To embody the consciousness or feeling that is anticipated from the experience of achieving the goal. When this is accomplished, the direction or action steps to move toward the completed vision come into play in the most effortless, joyful, and synchronistic ways. With virtually all my clients and students, meditation plays a most essential role in raising consciousness and is a consistent action step that ultimately leads one to live from an inner experience of freedom, love, and joy, which is the key to a fulfilling life on all levels.

In 2004, my wife and I traveled to India and visited many sacred sites and spent some time at the Sai Baba Ashram in Puttaparthi. I received a profound lesson there. I had been interested and intrigued by Sai Baba and his teachings for many years, not only because of the reports of the miracles that he performed in manifesting objects and other such phenomena but, more important because of the social services he had provided. A great deal of the prosperity garnered from his teachings was channeled into services to help the people of his impoverished country.

He created a college and hospital that were both free for his people. He funded irrigation projects to bring running water to villages that previously had none. He was clearly an example of living compassion and service for the good of all.

The ashram, which may sound like a small community where

people come to have an intimate spiritual experience, actually had anywhere from forty thousand to eighty thousand people staying at one time. I had never been in a group of even a hundred people who had such a unified intention, let alone the sixty thousand who were there when we were visiting. The intention was a clear focus on the teachings of Sai Baba, which are all about love, service, and honoring and revealing the common truths within all spiritual traditions and religions. What came to me while living and breathing in this constant vibration of love was a clearer and deeper understanding of who we really are and why we are all here. At the most basic level, we are all simply *love unfolding more love*.

My meditation practice has been consistent for most of my adult life as a daily practice averaging thirty minutes a day, five days a week. I remember a few times in my early twenties going a few months without meditating and returning to the practice to find that I had lost a great deal of the peace experienced when I was practicing consistently. The benefits of meditation are subtle, so while there may be some important, noticeable benefits early on in one's practice, the greater rewards are realized over time. In fact, because I have been meditating consistently for so long, I can't say for certain how much of my growth has been a result of the practice or simply wisdom and inner peace gained from life experience, but I would bet that I wouldn't have accomplished half of what I have in life if not for meditation and, more important, would not be living anywhere near the level of peace, prosperity, and joy that I am blessed to experience on a daily basis.

From 2000 to 2012, I served as president of the Spiritual Unity Movement, which offers meditation ceremonies each month at the time of the full moon, as well as other meditation offerings. I continue to serve on the advisory board and was awarded an honorary Doctorate of Divinity in 2010 from this organization.

I have also been involved in shamanic and indigenous teachings for more than thirty years and lead nontraditional sweat lodge ceremonies at my home once a month. I have been trained by several elders from different tribes in these practices, including Cree, Blackfoot, and Lakota. Since 1990, I have offered retreats in meditation and shamanic practices in various locations in the United States and Canada.

In offering meditation workshops, classes, and retreats over the past thirty years, I have developed a system for guiding people into deep meditative states, which tends to happen quite easily for most people. I use a variety of meditation techniques comprising ancient practices and specific modalities I have developed in my own meditation practice. Most participants experience a forty-minute to an hour-long meditation as lasting for ten to fifteen minutes. I will be offering the specific techniques I use in teaching meditation throughout the pages of this book, and I encourage you to go out and experience other classes, workshops, and group meditations to enhance your experience.

I am honored that you have chosen to read this book and look forward to meeting you on the inner planes and perhaps even in person sometime soon.

{ 1 }

WHAT IS MEDITATION?

Merriam-Webster's Dictionary's first definition of meditation is "a discourse intended to express its author's reflections or to guide others in contemplation."[1] That definition would make this book a meditation, but that isn't much help in describing the subject of this book—the practice of meditation. The second definition, "the act or process of meditating,"[2] is more appropriate for our subject, but it's still pretty vague, right? Okay, let's look at the definition for "meditating": "to engage in contemplation or reflection."[3] Now we're getting closer.

There may be as many definitions of meditation as there are meditation styles. I like to define meditation in a general way as any practice or activity that inspires a deep state of expanded awareness. With this definition, one can meditate while doing anything and everything. We don't have to have eyes closed to be in meditation. Walking meditation is a very common practice in the Buddhist tradition. In Vedic traditions (based on the ancient Vedic texts of India), the practice is to chant the name of God in the Sanskrit language throughout one's daily activities. While meditation can be done at any time and in any environment, the most common form and for most people the practice that inspires the deepest state is sitting meditation, usually with the eyes closed.

A more helpful published definition that validates my broader version is found in *The Free Dictionary*: "Meditation is a practice of focus upon a sound, object, visualization, the breath, movement, or attention itself in order to increase awareness of the present moment, reduce stress, promote relaxation, and enhance personal and spiritual growth."[4] I would add to that definition: to connect with or even surrender oneself into infinite light, love, and peace. To go beyond one's personal identification and be absorbed into the One. Sivanada Saraswati put it this way: "Meditation is the dissolution of thoughts into eternal awareness or pure consciousness without objectification, knowing without thinking, merging finitude in infinity."

One might say that a goal of meditation is to shift identification from the personal self to the transpersonal self, to use a term from "spiritual" or "transpersonal" psychology. The essence of who we are beneath the level of personal identification has been called by many names: soul, Atma, higher self, Tao within, eternal self, Buddha nature, authentic self, inner wisdom, nonlocal self, expanded self. Each of these terms represents our infinite, indestructible nature. It is the part of us, or really the whole of us, that never dies and knows our past and future. At the level of this identity, we are not separate individuals; we are all one. Virtually everyone who experiences deep meditation and who has communicated his or her findings shares this experience of touching their essence, soul, and true self.

The point of meditation is not simply to sit and enjoy a relaxed or even altered state for the duration of the meditation, although that alone can be incentive enough in our busy lives. It is to transform consciousness over time——to ultimately have the awareness gained from inward exploration become a lasting part of daily experience. The intention is to maintain as much as possible the peace, calm, lightness, and oneness that can be realized throughout the entire day or days until the next meditation session.

While meditation can be done any time and in any environment, the most common form, and for most people the practice that inspires the deepest state, is sitting meditation. It might be helpful to differentiate the two most common styles of meditation as mindfulness meditation or open monitoring meditation (a scientific term), and what I will call still-mind meditation, or attention-focused meditation (to use another scientific term).

MINDFULNESS MEDITATION, which can include Vipassana, Zen, and other related Buddhist forms, is geared toward awareness in the present moment. We simply notice and observe whatever we are experiencing without judgment. We don't try to get rid of or even transcend thoughts, feelings, noises, sensations, or awareness. We simply observe these experiences. By becoming the observer, we gain a perspective beyond that of personal identification. In some cases, mindfulness meditation may include some of the techniques from still-mind meditation, such as watching the breath, reciting inner mantras, etc., but in a classical sense, mindfulness meditation fits the description of focused-attention meditation.

STILL-MIND MEDITATION, which is associated with various Vedic practices from the ancient East Indian scriptures, aims to quiet the mind completely by focusing on one specific thing only, such as the breath, a mantra, an image, etc. In the yogic traditions, it has been said that if one can still the mind and go without any thoughts for three minutes or more (in my experience, it's not exact timing), one will reach a state of samadhi—pure bliss. Revered guru and author of more than two hundred books on Vedanta and yoga Swami Sivananda says, "In samadhi, or superconsciousness, the meditator's senses, mind, and intellect cease functioning. Just as the river joins the ocean, the individual mixes with the Supreme Soul. All limitations and differences disappear. The meditator attains the highest knowledge and eternal bliss."

I have experienced extended moments of this state on occasion during my meditative practices and can attest that it is profound. On other occasions, my mind cycles in and out of still mind or pure bliss, which can also be profound as long as I'm not judging my experience as lacking because it isn't completely still mind. This is another definition of meditation I find quite useful, not only the act of being in still mind or deep mindfulness, but the act of moving in and out of deep, still mind.

If we believe that we are only meditating when we are experiencing still mind or a deep state of mindfulness, then it's likely we'll get frustrated at our inability to do so. In teaching meditation classes and workshops, I've found that participants often find this expanded definition helpful. Many who have tried and given up meditation do so because it just seems too hard to let the thoughts go or even to observe them mindfully. In the "Helpful Hints" section of chapter 3 and in the guided meditations in chapter 4, I present techniques to make deep mindfulness and still mind easier, even effortless, for most people. If we are judging ourselves for not doing it right, we will not be in a state conducive to meditation.

Everyone who has ever meditated has encountered the seemingly never-ceasing analytical mind, which is often called "monkey mind" for its ability to jump around from tree to tree or, in this case, from thought to thought, never stopping. When the Dalai Lama struggles with meditation, his struggle (although it isn't called "struggle" when we accept it) is the same as yours and mine. My encouragement is to recognize that you *are* meditating as long as you are moving in and out of still or quiet mind, even if the stillness lasts for just one second. By giving up judgment and continuing to practice, meditators usually find that the cycles of stillness will increase and the moments of monkey mind decrease. In acceptance, the struggle evaporates and simply becomes practice.

The two basic forms of meditation are quite intertwined, as they originate from the same Vedic sources. The nonjudgmental observation of mindfulness meditation was in a sense added to the older practices of still-mind meditation as a result of Buddhist influence. My greatest experiences in meditation are when I am resting in pure bliss and connecting with Infinite Reality beyond the realm of thought arrived at through still-mind meditation. But, once again, everyone is different and will resonate with different styles and specific forms. And you don't have to stick to only one practice. One can in fact employ as many techniques as feel right. Some teachers would argue this point and say it is far better to find one practice and stick with it, and that too can be a personal preference.

Ultimately, I employ both of these forms, as do many others. For example, I use mindfulness to come to a point of pure presence, nonresistance, and nonjudgment, and then slip into still mind using the still-mind techniques illustrated below of watching the breath, and most often, silent mantra. As thoughts come in, observe them and/or invite them in and surrender again into the stillness until the next thought presents itself. Observe that thought, invite it in, and once again surrender into the pure bliss of no-thought. Once again, these are the two most common forms of meditation, but there are many other related forms described in the two sections below.

HISTORY OF MEDITATION

We have no way of knowing exactly how long meditation was practiced before there were verifiable records. Some scholars and archaeologists believe meditation may have been around as early as 5000 BCE. The earliest records of meditation, called Dhyana, from the Vedanta Hindu traditions, are from around 1500 BCE. These Vedic texts, or Vedas, outline various meditation forms and basic philosophies that are the hallmark of Hinduism and other Vedic traditions, including Taoism, Buddhism, Sikhism, and more modern spiritual systems, such as Theosophy, New Age, New Thought, transpersonal psychology, and medical applications. In fact, virtually all modern forms of meditation have been influenced by Vedanta meditation to some degree.

There are four Vedas, all of which discuss various aspects of meditation and the spiritual life: Rigveda, Yajurveda, Samaveda, and Atharvaveda. Each Veda is subclassified into four major text types: the Samhitas (mantras and benedictions), the Aranyakas (texts on rituals, ceremonies, and sacrifices), the Brahmanas (commentaries on rituals, ceremonies, and sacrifices), and the Upanishads (texts discussing meditation, philosophy, and spiritual knowledge).

Buddhism is predicated on the teachings of Siddhartha Gautama, known as Gautama Buddha. Scholars debate the exact origins of Buddhist meditation in its formalized fashion, although the early followers of the Buddha were certainly using some form of meditation as part of their practice. Early records of the various practices and states of meditation in Buddhism are described in the Pali Canon, which is dated in the first century BCE.

Buddhist meditation encompasses a variety of meditation techniques that aim to develop sati (mindfulness), samadhi (concentration), abhijna (supramundane powers), samatha (tranquility), and Vipassana (insight). It is generally accepted that there are about 350 million Buddhists worldwide today. However, if you include those who do not identify themselves as Buddhists but practice mindfulness meditation, that number is much larger.

Bodhidharma was a Buddhist monk credited with bringing Chan Buddhism to China in the fifth or sixth century, which led to the oriental forms of Buddhism, including Mahayana and Zen. He also began the physical training of the Shaolin monks in kung fu, which is also considered a form of Buddhism.

Other forms of meditation were developed through Taoism in China and Buddhism in India and spread to other countries in the Orient. Taoist meditation focuses on concentration, mindfulness, contemplation, and visualization and is in many ways intertwined with Buddhist meditation practices. Chinese medicine and martial arts adapted specific Taoist meditative techniques, including Neidan (internal alchemy) and Qigong (movement and breathing).

There is evidence that meditation existed in some form in Judaism, as indicated by the Torah, specifically in Genesis, which is understood to have been written in the fifth or sixth century BCE, which means that the practices must have existed earlier than that time.

Philo of Alexandria, a Hellenistic Jewish philosopher in Rome, introduced meditation methods in the first century BCE. There are various traditional forms of Jewish meditation, including visualization, emotional insight in communitive prayer, and analysis of philosophical, ethical, and/or mystical concepts. It can also be combined with unstructured prayer.

Kabbalah, the mystical branch of Judaism, includes a clear and robust meditative teaching. In the thirteenth century, Abraham Abulafia founded the school of Prophetic/Ecstatic Kabbalah and wrote meditation manuals using Hebrew letters and words to achieve ecstatic states.

Another contributor to meditative exploration in the West included Plotinus, one of the influential Greek philosophers who developed meditative techniques in the third century. He was clearly a mystic who fully understood the point of meditation. From personal experience, he believed a person could reach a "blank state" of no thought where he or she could merge with The One and the personality could dissolve into the Monad. Plotinus (as well as virtually all post-Platonic Greek philosophers) was influenced by Plato, who was also a proponent of deep contemplation.

Meditation in Christianity started to become prevalent in the twelfth century and even more so in the fourteenth century. In contrast to Eastern meditation practices, traditional Christian meditation most often engages the mind in reflecting on biblical passages and prayers, rather than on quieting or even silencing the mind. The more notable proponents of Christian meditation were Saint Thomas Aquinas (1225–1274); Saint Ignatius of Loyola (1491–1556), founder of the Jesuits; Saint Teresa of Avila (1515–1582), one of the most celebrated of Christian mystics; Saint John of the Cross (1542–1591), a close friend of Saint Teresa's; and Saint Padre Pio (1887–1968).

There are less traditional and more mystical expressions of Christian meditation as well, and in more recent times, Christianity too has been influenced by Eastern teachings on meditation, so in Christian communities, you can find many forms of meditation classes. Saint Teresa describes the four stages of mystical prayer:

1. **Meditation or contemplation:** This stage involves meditating on the life of Jesus Christ and engendering one's love for him. This fits the more traditional definition of Christian meditation.

2. **The Prayer of Quiet:** While meditating [in Christian terms] can be taken upon by your own volition, the prayer of quiet is entered by God's volition. Grace is revealed and a degree of union with God is achieved. This stage and the following two are more aligned with the Eastern and, specifically, Vedic definition of meditation although not called meditation by Saint Teresa.

3. **Union:** Your faculties become completely quiet and your soul is absorbed by God. Even your body shares in the soul's joy and delight.

4. **Rapture:** All your faculties fade away and the Lord gathers up your soul. Your hearing and thinking are dimmed and you are carried away gently, joyfully, silently, ecstatically. When Saint Teresa would reach this state, she was said to levitate and her nun colleagues would literally have to hold her body down.

After writing the above description of rapture (which in my estimation is synonymous with the Eastern samadhi) yesterday, this morning's meditation went deeper than usual. I am currently teaching a class for the second time based on the teachings of Saint Teresa and found her descriptions of mystical experience extremely inspiring.

The Modern Era

The transcendentalists were notable philosophers and writers of the early nineteenth century, including Ralph Waldo Emerson,

Henry David Thoreau, Margaret Fuller, Amos Bronson Alcott, Frederic Henry Hedge, and Theodore Parker. They were influenced by Eastern thought and practice and proponents of meditation as a means to higher consciousness. There is a connection between the transcendentalists and the Unitarian (now called Unitarian Universalist) movement. Emerson was a Unitarian minister, although he later moved on from traditional religion as his philosophical explorations evolved. It is likely that the transcendentalists influenced the use of meditation in Unitarianism, which has also been influenced by Eastern forms because of the eclectic nature of the denomination.

The practices of Eastern yoga and meditation were introduced in a dynamic way to the United States by Swami Vivekananda in the late 1800s. He gave a short but famous speech representing India and Hinduism at the Parliament of the World's Religions on September 11, 1893. After that event he toured extensively in the United States, sharing meditation and yoga techniques. He founded the Vedanta Society of New York in 1894.

Emanuel Swedenborg (who inspired the New Church, founded in 1787, fifteen years after his death), the transcendentalists, and Franz Mesmer ("the father of hypnosis") were all influencers of the New Thought movement, not to be confused with New Age. Phineas Quimby is considered to be the founder of New Thought. In 1840, he began to use Mesmer's techniques for healing. New Thought pioneers included Charles and Myrtle Fillmore (founders of Unity, or Unity Church, in 1891), Emma Curtis Hopkins ("the teacher of teachers"), Joel Goldsmith, Emmet Fox, Ernest Holmes (the founder of Religious Science), and, more recently, Jean Houston, Louise Hay, Terry Cole-Whittaker, Edwene Gaines, Michael Beckwith (founder of Agape International), Esther and Jerry Hicks (Abraham Teachings), Ken Gordon (spiritual leader of Centers for Spiritual Living), and many others who have been strong promoters of meditation, which continues to be practiced within New Thought communities. New Thought is eclectic in its philosophical beliefs and practices and has also been strongly influenced by the mystical traditions of the East as well as metaphysical interpretations of the Bible.

Theosophy was a prevalent movement in the late 1800s and early 1900s, started by Helena Blavatsky, a Russian mystic. Her epic treatise, *The Secret Doctrine*, drew from many of the world's most ancient scriptures and galvanized their messages into one comprehensive system. Theosophy influenced the Alice Bailey teachings (which highly emphasize group meditation and various esoteric methods), the I AM teachings, and other movements, all of which were precursors to what became popularized as the New Age movement, and all of which heavily emphasize meditation as the primary means of personal and spiritual transformation.

The New Age movement (not to be confused with New Thought) is believed to have originated in the early 1970s and is a nonorganized (in the sense that there is no central organization) network of individuals and businesses who believe we are at a pivotal point in history, embarking on a major, global paradigm shift based on the progression from the Piscean Age to the Aquarian Age. The movement was also influenced by notable authors and visionaries, such as Emanuel Swedenborg, Franz Mesmer, Buckminster Fuller, Marilyn Ferguson, Barbara Marx Hubbard, Jane Roberts, David Spangler, Shirley MacLaine, and many others. In the 1980s, it became a huge fad with hundreds of thousands in attendance at expos and conventions. It was so popular and marketable that many entrepreneurs identified their businesses with the movement for economic advantage and, in most cases, for philosophical alignment as well. It even birthed the genre of New Age music, with meditative and relaxing tones as its hallmark. Eventually the fad status led to loss of credibility and progressively more individuals and businesses disassociated from the term "New Age." Even *New Age Journal*, which was highly successful under that moniker, changed its name to *Body & Soul* magazine.

There are still many who identify as New Agers (and even more who are immersed in the practices and philosophy and may not identify with the name), and most who do are meditators. There are many similarities between New Age and New Thought, although there are some strong philosophical differences. Both emphasize our essential unity, the mystical practice of experiencing the Divine, and spiritual practice and meditation as a means of personal and transformational growth and are very accessible today for meditation groups, classes, and training.

Meditation has also played a role in modern psychology. Carl Jung, William James, and Roberto Assagioli are considered early influencers of what eventually became the field of transpersonal psychology (more recently oftentimes called spiritual psychology) early in the twentieth century. All three of these celebrated psychologists were open to and proponents of meditation (in various forms) as a means of psychological healing. James said: "The faculty of voluntarily bringing back a wandering attention over and over again, is the very root of judgment, character, and will."

Carl Jung developed a therapeutic intervention called active imagination. Some meditative purists would not consider this a form of meditation, but using the wider definition of any practice that leads to an altered and enhanced state of awareness, active imagination certainly qualifies. In this process, the contents of the unconscious are objectified as images, a narrative, or personified as individualized aspects or personalities of the self. The subject allows the rational mind to become less active as images and feelings emerge to gain clarity and ultimately heal unconscious elements of the self.

Assagioli, a contemporary of Freud and Jung, developed one of the most fundamentally spiritual forms of psychology, called "psychosynthesis," which emphasizes the synthesis of all aspects of personality, including the transpersonal or higher unconscious and the lower unconscious or shadow self. To this end, visualization, meditation, and extensions of active imagination are employed. Assagioli was also a mystic who studied Theosophy, Eastern philosophy, and the Alice Bailey teachings. He founded two groups intended to teach meditation and New Age philosophy. His written work developed specific meditation techniques, including reflective, receptive, and creative meditation.

In the 1960s, transpersonal psychology, which emerged from humanistic psychology (founded by Carl Rogers), became a legitimate branch of psychology that includes spiritual and transcendent aspects of human experience. Some of the pioneers in this field, all proponents of meditation as a means of personal and spiritual growth, include Ken Wilber, who created a form of mindfulness meditation called "integral mindfulness"; Robert Frager, the founder of the Institute of Transpersonal Psychology, who integrated Sufism (the mystical branch of Islam) with psychology; Daniel Goleman, who wrote several books on Buddhism and emotional intelligence and *The Science of Meditation: How to Change Your Brain, Mind, and Body*; Roger Walsh, who integrated meditation, shamanic practices, and other spiritual practices from many different traditions into transpersonal psychology; John Welwood, writer of several books on integrating Western psychology with Eastern wisdom; and Charles Tart, a prolific writer on human transformation, including a seminal book entitled *Mind Science: Meditation Training for Practical People*.

In the 1960s, there was an explosion of interest in meditation fueled by Maharishi Mahesh Yogi and his system of Transcendental Meditation, or TM. He taught this system to thousands of individuals through world tours from 1958 to 1965. The well-documented participation of the Beatles and other celebrities in this technique was a major influence in the popularization of the practice. Maharishi created many training centers around the world, and by the turn of this century, millions had been taught this system.

Ram Das, formerly Richard Alpert, along with Timothy Leary and others were pioneers of psychedelic research and experimentation in the early 1960s for the purpose of higher consciousness. In 1967, becoming disillusioned with the limitations of psychotropic drugs, Alpert traveled to India searching for alternatives to higher consciousness and met his guru, Neem Karoli Baba, also known as Maharishi Mahariji, who gave him the name Ram Das. He returned to America to share what he had learned through his bestselling book, *Be Here Now*, in 1971 and subsequent lecturing, as well as many other bestsellers, all of which were influential in the expansion of the growing meditation movement in the United States.

The recent popularity of mindfulness meditation is generally attributed to Jon Kabat-Zinn, a professor at the University of Massachusetts Medical School. In 1979, he founded the Mindfulness-Based Stress Reduction Program to treat the chronically ill. He combined the practices of yoga and meditation with scientific research and created a program that is used by medical practitioners, medical centers, and hospitals to help with stress, anxiety, pain, and illness.

Because meditation has been gradually going mainstream over the past several decades, today there are many organizations, companies, and corporations, large and small, who offer meditation training for their employees to help manage stress and improve performance. The following are well-known organizations that have meditation training programs: Google, Target,

Facebook, Twitter, eBay, Intel, Nike, LinkedIn, General Mills, Reebok, Yahoo!, Apple, AOL, HBO, Procter & Gamble, Columbia Business School, Harvard University, Stanford Graduate School, Drucker School of Management, Michigan's Ross School of Business, UC Berkeley Haas School of Business, and of course, many others.

Some of the most popular and recent proponents of meditation include the Dalai Lama, Thich Nhat Hanh, Sai Baba, Pema Chödrön, Swami Satchidananda, Eckhart Tolle, Jack Kornfield, Deepak Chopra, Caroline Myss, Marianne Williamson, and Michael Singer, to name a few. Deepak Chopra and Oprah Winfrey have teamed up to periodically offer a widely popular twenty-one-day meditation series.

There are also countless proponents of meditation for enhanced athletic performance. Phil Jackson, the most winning coach of all time, taught meditation techniques to his championship basketball teams. Seattle Seahawks coach Pete Carroll attributed their Super Bowl win in part to the players meditating. Sri Chinmoy, a well-known meditation teacher, credited meditation and grace for his unparalleled success in athleticism. A champion sprinter and decathlete in his youth, at age fifty-four he took up weightlifting. He went from lifting forty pounds with one hand to setting world records two years later by lifting one-handed more than three and a half tons (7,063¾ pounds to be exact, equivalent to six small elephants) a few inches off the support braces that held the weights. Of his feat, he said: "I give not 99 percent, but 100 percent of credit for my lifting to my Lord's compassion. It is his grace alone that is enabling me to be of inspiration to the world like this."

Many successful athletes are meditators, some of whom are listed here, along with well-known meditators in various fields of endeavor: Albert Einstein, Sir Isaac Newton, Benjamin Franklin,

Walt Whitman, Mick Jagger, David Lynch, Bruce Lee, Tiger Woods, Hugh Jackman, Goldie Hawn, Clint Eastwood, Harrison Ford, George Harrison, Paul McCartney, John Lennon, Michael Jordan, George Lucas, Jerry Seinfeld, Phil Jackson, Kobe Bryant, LeBron James, Misty May-Treanor, Kerri Walsh Jennings, Herbie Hancock, William Ford Jr., Sting, Allen Ginsberg, Cher, Mark Wahlberg, and Sheryl Crow.

SPECIFIC TYPES OF MEDITATION

There are many types and styles of meditation. I will list some of the more common ones and offer simple definitions, but the complete list is far longer. When I offer meditation classes and workshops, I guide meditations using many of the styles I list here. Everyone is unique, and one technique or style may work effectively for one person and not at all for another. The Meditation Sampler guided meditation in chapter 4, "Meditation Practice," is a replica of the format I use in my trainings. Try various styles until you find one that resonates. Over time you may add other elements or styles to your meditation.

My daily practice, having evolved over forty-two years, includes several different techniques I have used over the years, including the Color Cycle, mentioned in the introduction of this book; visualizing a place in nature in my mind and planning my day with the various aspects of myself (called "subpersonalities" in spiritual psychology); focusing my attention on three specific symbols in the area of the third eye, the point between and slightly above the brows; and dissolving into quiet mind for fifteen to twenty minutes or more. I also incorporate chanting and/or inner mantras and recite a World Prayer called "The Great Invocation" (a prayer of ancient origin published in the Alice

Baily teachings); and finally I finish by offering distance energy healing for people I know who have requested prayer or healing as well as for close family and friends. That's a lot of elements, right? Others who practice techniques like silent mantra, which was popularized by Transcendental Meditation, have but one primary technique—repeating an inner mantra. Whether you ultimately practice one technique or many, you can experiment with some of the styles below to find what works best for you.

Mindfulness Meditation

Mindfulness meditation originated in the Buddhist tradition. Mindfulness is a primary principle in Buddhist teachings and is believed to lead to enlightenment. There are many forms of Buddhist meditation, and all of them are predicated on mindfulness.

The primary component of mindfulness meditation is to simply notice what you notice. In contradistinction to mantra, chanting, and breathing techniques designed to quiet the mind (and used in some forms of mindfulness meditation), in mindfulness meditation, the mind is used to increase awareness and be fully present in the moment without judgment.

While sitting in mindfulness meditation (as opposed to walking or other activities), you become aware of whatever presents itself. If you notice a tension in your body, you simply observe that sensation without judgment or resistance. In some practices, you could breathe into the tension, not to make it go away, but to fully embrace it. Of course, once we give up resistance to anything, it tends to dissipate. Resistance magnifies discomfort, embracing dissipates. This is one of many examples of how meditation is a metaphor for life.

When a feeling is noticed, it is simply observed without judgment or resistance. When a thought comes into play, it is watched without judgment or resistance. If a thought about a feeling or thought emerges from the observation, that too becomes the subject of watching.

I was practicing this form recently, and some interesting realizations occurred. It was during a silent meditation augmented by the sweet sound of an acoustic guitar being played by the leader. As the meditation progressed, I noticed that when I was lost in my thoughts, or simply not aware that my mind was drifting off on some journey of thinking, I would be only aware of those thoughts as they unfolded. When I observed my thoughts, I would also be aware of the sound of the guitar, the others in the room, the sound of someone writing, other sounds, virtually the entire experience—mindfulness.

Then I decided to observe the consciousness observing my thoughts. I experienced an even more dynamic expansiveness of awareness and stillness. I then decided to observe the consciousness observing the consciousness observing my thoughts. At this point, I went beyond all sense of thought and observation and into completely still mind without thought at all for long periods of time. If a thought did come into play, it quickly dissolved into the pure bliss I was experiencing.

Vipassana, or insight meditation, is a form of mindfulness meditation and is present in virtually all Buddhist practices. This form has become quite prevalent in recent decades through the Vipassana movement, popularized by Mahasi Sayadaw. There are many schools and independent teachers of this form that usually offer ten- or thirty-day retreats. Modern Vipassana focuses primarily on scanning the body, sometimes in sections, and observing its functions as a metaphor for the impermanence of all things physical and leading to insight and, ultimately, enlightenment.

Zen is another popular form within the scope of mindfulness meditation and is specific to the Japanese Buddhist tradition. Zen

Dhyana (meditation) specifically uses watching the breath and breath-counting techniques as described in "Breathing Techniques" in this book. This specific form of sati or mindfulness also includes observing one's thoughts.

As in still-mind meditation, mindfulness meditation is not designed only to inspire the peace that comes during meditation but to sustain the meditation practice through daily living. On the road to enlightenment, we become more and more present in the moment and increasingly mindful about the vibration and qualities of thought, behavior, and speech. Ultimately, we translate our inner peace into our outer lives.

There is a mindfulness exercise designed to illustrate this dynamic with a specific physical activity. The traditional exercise is to slowly eat a raisin (or other type of sweet fruit) and engross yourself completely in the activity. Observe the color of the fruit as you prepare to take a bite. Smell its fragrance. Be aware of your mouth opening to take a bite. While biting and slowly chewing, be fully present to the taste and texture of the fruit as you chew and swish it around in your mouth. Fully observe the sensation of swallowing. Perhaps even intuit the organs receiving the fruit and beginning the process of absorbing its nutrients. One can find this dynamic occurring naturally while eating at a silent retreat. When the distractions of the world are reduced, we naturally adapt to a state of mindfulness.

Silent Mantra

Silent mantra existed in different forms before Transcendental Meditation was developed and promoted by Maharishi Mahesh Yogi in the 1950s. What makes TM unique as a form of silent mantra is that each participant is given their own personalized mantra that they take away and can use for the rest of their lives.

You can also practice silent mantra by formulating your own

or using different mantras at various times for myriad purposes. The popular meditation offered by Oprah Winfrey and Deepak Chopra uses a different Sanskrit mantra each morning for twenty-one days. Hindu and other Vedic traditions use Sanskrit words in chants, because the language has a high vibration and was developed purely for communication of spiritual concepts.

A self-formulated mantra can be as simple as "I am light, I am love, I am pure peace" or perhaps sounding an inner tone like the Om or Aum, both Sanskrit names for the Divine or First Cause. In the beginning was the word (according to the Bible), and the word was "Aum" (according to Vedic texts). Personally, I find a constant inner tone of the "Ah" sound, sung kind of like how you would imagine the voices of angels, takes me to that deep state of quiet mind far more effectively than any other technique. Many in my meditation trainings also find this technique extremely helpful. If you want to try out this practice, you can find it as part of the Meditation Sampler beginning on page 67.

Breathing Techniques

There are many different breathing techniques that have evolved from ancient practices designed to quiet the mind and/or facilitate a state of mindfulness. The most common is watching the breath. The meditator simply watches the breath as it goes in and out. Most commonly the inhalation is through the nose and exhalation through the mouth, creating a circle of breathing. Everything in life is cyclic in nature, so by employing this kind of breathing, we are in harmony with the natural way of life.

Taken a step further, one can focus on the points between the in breath and the out breath. These in-between points represent perfect balance and can lead one to the place of nonduality. Symbolically, they are the points between receiving and giving, positive and negative, yin and yang, light and dark, death and life, manifestation and dissolution, feminine and masculine, spirit and matter, Mother Earth and Father Sky. If you want to try out this kind of meditation practice, you can find it as part of the Meditation Sampler beginning on page 67.

There are several deep-breathing meditation techniques that involve counting, and the counts may vary from system to system. The four-seven-eight method is quite common. Breathe in through the nose to the count of four, hold the breath to the count of seven, and breathe out through the mouth to the count of eight. The counting is done quite slowly, like one count per second. You can also experiment with finding your own counting rhythm that works best for you or let go of the counting completely and simply find the rhythm that feels most natural. If you find yourself getting dizzy, which can happen, stop the deep breathing, return to normal breathing, and then begin again when you are ready.

When practicing deep breathing techniques of any kind, it is recommended to do what is called abdominal breathing as opposed to chest breathing. This involves expanding your abdomen when you breathe, so you are breathing deep into your lungs. If you feel your chest rising as you breathe, you know your breath is shallow. The breathing of most people is shallow. For optimal health, this form of deep breathing can be done at all times, not just while meditating.

Chanting

Virtually every cultural and religious system uses a form of chanting or singing as a means of spiritual development. Some forms are more vibrant and can include movement as well, while others are more clearly focused on leading to an inner, quiet meditative state.

Some of the more prevalent forms of chanting include Vedic Sanskrit, of which Kirtan is a common practice; Western styles, most notably Gregorian and Jewish cantillation; and that of aboriginal cultures, such as Native Americans, First Nations people of Canada, Hawaiian kahunas, Native Africans, Australian Aboriginals, Central and South American tribes, and many more.

Vedic chanting is based on the ancient Vedic texts and uses the sacred language of Sanskrit. I find in meditation trainings if no other method is effective in stilling the mind, then Vedic chanting does the trick for most people. The Vedic Sanskrit language was created to communicate spiritual concepts and therefore has a very high frequency of vibration. Any kind of chanting can be effective, but I find that using specific Sanskrit mantras are most effective for meditation. The Hare Krishna movement uses Vedic Sanskrit chanting as well. In group sessions, this form can be quite vibrant and accompanied by fervent dancing, which can lead one into a trance state. In my early twenties, I lived a couple of blocks from a Hare Krishna center and loved to take part in their free vegetarian meals followed by the ceremony.

Kirtan, or Kirtana, is a specific type of Vedic chanting that is usually done in a group ceremony and is most often a call-and-response style using devotional names of various Vedic deities. Hindus and other Vedic traditions use the Sanskrit chants to sing the names of gods while going about daily activities as an effective means of holding the intention of devotion throughout the day.

Native American and First Nations chanting is used primarily in various ceremonies of tribal peoples that in recent times are often open to people of nonnative descent. These ceremonies include sweat lodges (which have become quite common in the New Age movement, men's movement, and other modern-day Western gatherings), powwows, sun dances, and many others. Combined with drumming, these chants effectively induce an altered state of consciousness, enhancing the "medicine" of the ceremonies for healing and communion with Wakan Tanka, which is Lakota for "Great Spirit" or the "Great Mystery," and all aspects of nature.

Gregorian chanting is the sacred song of the Roman Catholic Church developed mainly in the ninth and tenth centuries AD. These chants are most often sung in church by priests, choirs, and sometimes whole congregations and were developed to create a sacred state of mind during mass and other ceremonies. Chanting and song can be found in the earliest expressions of Christianity.

Jewish cantillation is the ritual chanting of readings from the Hebrew Bible in Jewish ceremonies. The cantor is an essential player in the sacred ceremonies, sometimes considered as essential as the rabbi. These melodic songs also enhance a state of sacredness in the ceremonies.

Yoga

When people in the West hear the term "yoga," it most likely will bring up images of people in various positions for physical strengthening, stretching, and general health. Hatha yoga focuses on physical development and traditionally includes a meditative focus. The meditation aspect of the practice may be emphasized more or less, depending on the particular teacher and whether you experience it at a yoga studio, gym, or private practice.

Yoga originated in ancient India as early as the sixth century BCE and is a traditional practice in many Eastern religions, including Jainism, Buddhism, Hinduism, Sikhism, and other Vedic traditions. Hatha yoga is just one of many different yogic practices. Some of the other more prevalent forms are:

- **KARMA YOGA** is the yoga of action. One purifies all actions in the world and offers them as gifts to Divine Beings.

- **RAJA YOGA** is known as the yoga of knowledge and focuses on controlling the mind and body and may be combined with hatha yoga to attain enlightenment and emphasizes meditative practice.

- **BHAKTI YOGA** is the yoga of devotion and emphasizes love for all things. Chanting the names of the Vedic deities as a form of worship and devotion is the most prevalent practice.

- **JNANA YOGA** is considered the most difficult of the yogic paths and is not undertaken without a certain degree of mastery of the other three paths discussed. Its ultimate aim is complete unification with God.

- **KRIYA YOGA** is a specific yogic practice focused on breathing, developed by Paramahansa Yogananda as one of many Pranayama (yogic breathing) techniques.

- **TANTRIC YOGA** is known primarily in the West as a system for combining sexual practices with spiritual intention. Sexual and sensual acts are performed not purely for pleasure, but as a means to spiritual growth and enlightenment. Historically, however, tantra is much broader and refers to many forms of spiritual study and ritualistic practices in the Vedic traditions.

Meditation and Movement

As in the other forms, there are a multitude of ways in which movement and meditation are combined. Meditation while moving won't take most people quite as deep as sitting meditation, yet the benefits are great. On the other hand, I have had many students tell me that meditation movement works better for them than sitting meditation. Again, we are all different. Ahead are various common forms of meditation and movement, including one designed specifically by me.

WALKING MEDITATION is a simple form of meditation and

movement. Thich Nhat Hanh, a renowned Vietnamese Buddhist monk, and many others have been proponents of this practice in modern times. Springing primarily from the Buddhist tradition, the protocol is to walk slowly and be mindful of everything experienced on the walk. It's especially helpful to practice this form in a beautiful nature place. While walking, be aware of everything that is experienced—the sights, sounds, feelings, sensations, breeze on the face—while observing the thoughts that come up about the entire experience. This practice can be done in just a few minutes or for hours. If you want to try out walking meditation, you can find a guideline on page 79.

THE LABYRINTH is a specific form of walking meditation where the walking meditator enters a mazelike structure. It is only mazelike in the sense that it has a winding path with breaks that ultimately lead to the center. Unlike a maze, the labyrinth does not have dead ends to trick and confuse. Images of the labyrinth have been found in many lands on several continents and are commonly associated with Greek mythology. The earliest carvings, however, were found in a petroglyph in India in 2500 BCE. In medieval times, the labyrinth became a common part of cathedral architecture. The practice of walking the labyrinth has become popular in recent times, and labyrinths can be found at Christian sanctuaries of various denominations. The journey involves simply walking through and around the circles that lead to the center and back out again slowly and mindfully, inspiring reflection and receptivity to enhanced awareness of spiritual understanding or revelation.

WHIRLING DERVISH is a term you have probably heard that comes from Sufism, the mystical branch of Islam. It was invented by the world-famous poet Rumi, whose poems are among the most translated and published of any poet in the world. In the grief of the mysterious death of his great friend and teacher,

Shams-e-Tabrizi, Rumi found that slowly turning around a pillar would woo him into a meditative state. This evolved into the dervish practice of spinning around at great speeds.

The Universal Dances of Peace are also derived from Sufism. They were introduced in the 1960s by Samuel L. Lewis, who was influenced by Hazrat Inayat Khan, a Sufi master. They consist of circle dances and chants from all different cultures and religions for the purpose of meditation and honoring all paths to God. There is generally a leader who teaches the dances and chants and musicians playing acoustic guitars, tablas, or other drums and instruments.

TAI CHI is an ancient form of slow martial arts. It is used less for combat and more often (especially in modern times) for health and well-being. It is an excellent form of slow-movement meditation modeling the movements of animals.

QIGONG is also an ancient Chinese practice related to and considered part of Tai Chi, which is used for healing oneself and is performed as a meditative form. Qigong practice typically involves moving meditation, coordinating slow-flowing movement, deep rhythmic breathing, and a calm meditative state of mind.

THE ATHLETE'S ZONE is a meditative state that is arrived at while performing sports. A well-documented expression of this phenomena is commonly called "runner's high." While long-distance running, athletes slip into a meditative state that allows them to increase performance and decrease the discomfort of the physical strain from the sport. Once the runner's high is reached, everything flows easily and effortlessly. It may appear as though everything around the runner seems to be moving in slow motion. Athletes in virtually all sports have reported this same experience. Basketball players report the game slows down; it may seem like the hoop is wider and shots simply cannot be missed.

Tennis players report that the racket feels three times larger and every shot is landed easily and effortlessly.

ZEN TENNIS is a practice I developed as a tennis pro in my early twenties. In most cases, the zone is something that occurs spontaneously. I developed a system for accessing this state purposely, which sprang from my own experience playing tennis, which I honed and taught to others and can be applied to any sport or experience. I include the instructions for this form in chapter 4, "Meditation Practice." If you want to try out this practice, you can find a guideline on page 81.

Drumming

Drumming is perhaps the oldest method for reaching meditative states. Since ancient times, tribal peoples sat in circles or around the fire making noise with sticks and stones and later crafted drums with wood frames and animal skins. Today, drum circles are a common form of music and can easily lead one into a meditative, if not mystical or trancelike, state. Some drum circles are spontaneous, where people gather and start drumming; others may be skillfully directed specifically for the purpose of meditation. Drums are used to augment other meditative musical forms, such as the tabla in Kirtan and other Middle Eastern ceremonies, native drums in chanting and tribal ceremonies, and many other percussion instruments from various cultures for the purpose of enhancing spiritual experience and various religious rites.

Guided Meditation and Visualization

The previously discussed techniques are designed to help one move into deep mindfulness and still the mind. Guided meditation stills the mind but not as potentially deeply as the modalities discussed, because guided meditation requires a more active mind to follow the guiding. It can be an excellent way to begin practice, though, and many beginners find it to be more comfortable because it is easier. Once some success is acquired from guided meditation, one can move on to more advanced practices, or use them concurrently.

With guided meditation, the guide generally takes the meditator on a journey to a relaxing, rejuvenating environment, such as a nature place, power spot, or sacred area, to experience healing and enlightened living. Oftentimes, people will slip into quiet or still mind during guided meditations and lose all track of the actual guiding. Some examples of guided meditation I have used include the following:

■ Finding a beautiful place in nature, such as a field of flowers, waterfall, mountain peak, or deserted island, that is designed to bring healing and regeneration. It contains the perfect energy for bringing your being back to perfect balance and harmony.

■ Traveling through the mountain ranges of Tibet to find an ancient temple deep in a forest and then entering the temple and sitting in the center of a cylinder of light.

■ Moving through the jungles of the Amazon to find a clearing where a sacred, ancient ritual is taking place and you are invited to join.

■ Walking through a crystal valley and venturing into the center of a giant quartz generator crystal.

■ Finding a natural altar in a sacred nature place and having a conversation with a wise being.

■ Floating down a river in a one-person boat, dragging your hand lazily in the water as you drift.

There are several examples of these types of guided meditation you can try out beginning on page 65.

Group Meditation

Group meditation can be done using any of the styles discussed. Most people find they are able to go deeper in meditation when meditating in a group, especially if the group is comprised of some experienced meditators. A field of consciousness is created, and the collective group consciousness helps to raise the vibration of everyone involved. You may also find that after meditating in a group, you can bring the experience back to your individual practice and find that it inspires a deeper experience on your own. As you begin your individual meditation, picture the members of the group you are regularly meditating with.

If you have a family, set aside a time each day or even once a week to meditate together. Imagine everyone—parents, children, grandparents if they are present—all turning off phones and spending a few moments of peaceful time together. Young children can meditate as well. In teaching his son of six to meditate, a friend of mine chose a stuffed rabbit and invited his son to gaze at it. They call it the "Meditation Bunny." His child and Meditation Bunny stare at each other and they both absolutely loved it!

{ 2 }

BENEFITS OF MEDITATION

As mentioned in the introduction, the full benefits of a regular meditation practice are subtle and realized over time. The best way to assess what you gain from meditation is to stop for a period of time after you've been practicing for a while. When I was first publishing *Meditation Magazine*, I was interviewed on a local TV show—my first—and was asked the question related to this chapter title: "What are the benefits of meditation?" The unprepared answer that flowed through my lips was "It's easier to describe what happens when I don't meditate. I forget the peace, the consistent attention to life purpose, the harmony, the love, the creativity that I enjoy while meditating consistently. Perhaps we can say that the practice of meditation is an act of remembering." Remembering who we truly are. Meditation is not only a means of becoming a better person, it is a path back to the source of our basic nature as being one with all things, all nature, an expression of the Divine.

HEALTH BENEFITS

Since the interest of meditation began to increase in the United States in 1959, there have been more than 600 studies done at more than 250 universities on the health benefits. Some of these studies have been discounted by the scientific community as being biased because of the researchers' affiliation with a meditation community, such as the many studies done on TM by researchers who were part of the TM movement. Other studies have been disregarded because of poor controls. This does not mean that there aren't indications of benefits in these studies; they just aren't widely accepted by the scientific community. On the other hand, there are many studies that are not discounted by bias or poor controls that were rigorous enough to stand the test of scientific scrutiny and that indicate specific and demonstrative benefits of meditation.

There is scientific evidence that meditation can be beneficial in the following areas: decreased memory loss, increased brain function and synchronization, improvement for post-traumatic stress disorder, lower cholesterol, pain reduction, improved immune function, healing for irritable bowel syndrome, reduced anxiety, reduced insomnia, decreased risk of stroke and heart disease, lower blood pressure, improved learning, reductions in depression, improved intelligence, improved emotional intelligence, quality of life in cancer patients, improved creativity, higher self-awareness, problem solving, and compassion for self and others. Next, we will examine several studies that are based on widely accepted research demonstrating some of the health benefits of meditation.

Prevention of Cognitive Decline

A study conducted at UCLA[1] between 2013 and 2015 indicated that Kundalini yoga not only proved to be effective in the treatment and prevention of cognitive decline, but was also more successful than standard memory-enhancement training used specifically for executive functioning and mood resilience.

The study included eighty-one participants divided into two groups. One group received Kundalini yoga training and the other standard memory-enhancement training. At twelve weeks and twenty-four weeks, both Kundalini yoga and memory-enhancement training groups showed significant improvement in memory; however, only the Kundalini yoga group showed significant improvement in executive functioning and reduced depressive symptoms and resilience at week twelve.

Healthy Brain Structure

There has been a high volume of studies indicating that brain structure is actually altered in positive ways through meditation. Isn't that amazing? One such study, led by Massachusetts General Hospital[2], showed that particular areas of the cerebral cortex, the outer layer of the brain, were thicker in participants who were experienced meditators in insight meditation. The twenty participants in the study averaged nine years of meditation experience and practiced about six hours per week. The control group of fifteen had no experience with meditation or yoga.

They found that the areas of the brain that were thicker and therefore functioning at a higher level were associated with heart rate, breathing, and the integration of emotion with thought and reward-based decision making—essentially one's capacity for emotional intelligence. They also found that regions of the brain associated with the integration of emotional and cognitive processes were thicker and more pronounced in older participants, which suggests that meditation can reduce the thinning of the cortex and associated mental decline that occurs with aging.

Pain Reduction

Multiple studies have proven that mindfulness meditation can significantly reduce pain, even with as little as three twenty-minute daily sessions. One such brain-related study conducted at Wake Forest School of Medicine in North Carolina[3] actually proved that not only does mindfulness meditation reduce pain, but, as demonstrated through MRI images, areas of the brain that affect pain are changed during and after meditation, eliminating any chance that the reduction in pain found in previous studies is the result of a placebo effect. The study showed that mindfulness meditation significantly deactivates the thalamus and periaqueductal gray matter, which facilitate low-level sensory and nerve-related processing. Particularly interesting is that this study was done with individuals who had no previous experience with meditation.

Brain and Immune Function Improvement

In a study titled "Alterations in Brain and Immune Function Produced by Mindfulness Meditation: Psychosomatic Medicine,"[4] twenty-five subjects in a work environment were offered a training program consisting of audio-recorded guided meditation for one hour per day, six days a week, for a period of eight weeks. This study was the first to indicate significant increases in left-side anterior activation of the brain that correspond with reduction of anxiety and increase in positive emotions. What is of particular significance is at the end of the eight-week period, subjects were vaccinated with influenza vaccine, and a significant increase in antibodies to the vaccine were recorded, indicating that regular meditation significantly strengthens the immune system. All the positive effects were compared to a control group that did not receive the meditation training and did not register the positive changes listed above.

Effective Treatment for Depression

Another study investigating meditation and brain function was introduced in a scientific paper entitled "Meditate Don't Medicate: How Medical Imaging Evidence Supports the Role of Meditation in the Treatment of Depression."[5] In this study, fifty-one different experiments that indicated changes in brain structure in meditators were reviewed for the purpose of exploring the effectiveness of meditation as treatment for depression.

Twelve of the fifty-one studies corroborated the theory that brain structure associated with depression is positively altered through meditative practice. Patients with depression are found to have neurotransmitter inhibition or decreased serotonin, noradrenaline, and dopamine, all of which are increased through the brain structures that are improved with meditation. Although the types of meditation used varied across the studies, the results from all studies were consistent, regardless of meditation style. One of the conclusions arrived at was that in a large number of cases, meditation is a superior form of treatment than medication because of the numerous side effects of the drugs used for treatment. Of course, in many other cases, medical treatment is appropriate, necessary, and can perhaps be augmented with meditation.

Stress, Cognitive Function, and Intelligence

A study entitled "Immediate and Long-term Effects of Meditation on Acute Stress Reactivity, Cognitive Functions, and Intelligence"[6] was conducted at the All India Institutes of Medical Sciences in New Delhi, India, with thirty-four healthy male students. The participants took part in a meditation session immediately after a stress phase, induced by playing a video game, to explore the immediate effects of meditation on acute-stress reactivity. The research team also explored the effects of the long-term practice of meditation on stress reactivity, intelligence, and cognitive functions, measured by standard intelligence quotient and Emotional Intelligence Quotient (EQ) tests.

In short-term results, galvanic skin response rose significantly during and after the stress phase and decreased slightly at the beginning of the meditation phase and significantly as the meditation period progressed. The reaction time, another measurement of stress, also improved dramatically after the meditation period. The long-term results after a month of meditation showed a decrease in galvanic skin response even during the stress phase compared to the testing at the beginning of the study. The long-term results also demonstrated a significant increase in IQ and EQ scores, indicating that regular long-term meditation results in an increase in intelligence and wisdom.

Increased Attention Ability

A study conducted at the University of Pennsylvania[7] by neuroscientist Amishi Jha and Michael Baime (director of Penn's Program for Mindfulness) investigated the effectiveness of mindfulness training in improving aspects of attention, including alerting—producing and maintaining a state of readiness to process environmental input; orienting—selecting the most relevant information from various inputs; and executive control function—resolving competing mental processes. These three aspects add up to one's capacity for rapid and accurate responses, or simply paying attention and responding effectively.

The study included three groups. One group consisted of individuals new to meditation who participated in an eight-week mindfulness-based stress reduction course (MBSR). A second group of individuals, experienced in meditation techniques, participated in a one-month intensive mindfulness retreat. The third group was a control group whose members had no training in meditation techniques.

All groups were tested for attention effectiveness at the beginning and end of the experiment. At the beginning, the experienced meditators participating in the retreat tested significantly higher in the alerting component of attention compared with those in the MBSR training and control group. At the end of the training, the MBSR training group had significantly improved in relation to the orienting component of attention compared with the retreat and control groups. The retreat group improved even more significantly in the altering component by the end of the retreat training. The executive control function of attention remained relatively the same in all three groups.

The results suggest that meditation mindfulness training may improve attention by enhancing specific functions of attention. The MBSR course improved the orientation component, and the retreat group improved in the alerting component.

Decreased Anxiety

In a study entitled "Effectiveness of a Meditation-Based Stress Reduction Program in the Treatment of Anxiety Disorders,"[8] twenty-two participants diagnosed with generalized anxiety disorder or panic disorder participated in a stress-reduction program based on mindfulness meditation. The study documented significant reductions in anxiety and depression scores in twenty of the twenty-one subjects. The number of participants experiencing panic symptoms was also reduced substantially. The positive results continued to be measured in a three-month and three-year follow-up. The study concluded that mindfulness meditation training can effectively reduce symptoms of anxiety and panic and maintain the reductions with continued practice.

HEALTH DETRIMENTS OF MEDITATION

With all these tremendous health benefits, are there any health liabilities resulting from meditation? In almost all cases, the answer is no. There are some rare exceptions that are mentioned in the following statement by the National Center for Complementary and Integrative Health:

> Meditation is considered to be safe for healthy people. There have been rare reports that meditation could cause or worsen symptoms in people who have certain psychiatric problems, but this question has not been fully researched. People with physical limitations may not be able to participate in certain meditative practices involving physical movement. Individuals with existing mental or physical health conditions should speak with their health care providers prior to starting a meditative practice and make their meditation instructor aware of their condition.

The only caution I would add for relatively emotionally and physically healthy individuals is to be mindful about not using meditation, or any spiritual practice for that matter, as a "spiritual bypass." It is very possible to use meditation or any spiritual practice inadvertently as a means for emotional suppression or avoidance of taking authentic action in our lives. It is important to express, and in some cases cathartically release, emotional wounds and also to face one's challenges and take action when needed, in addition to spiritual and meditation practices. In addition, I propose that an ongoing, consistent practice will ultimately lead one to a life of mindfulness and the inspiration to be present and authentic in all ways.

THE JOY FACTOR AND NONATTACHMENT

I cannot say to exactly what degree of influence meditation alone has contributed to living a life of joy, but I am certain that it has been highly significant. Other practices that have led to living in joy nearly every minute of every day include "radical gratitude," looking for the magic in every situation and recognizing that every challenge in life is never against us and always for us. This practice, along with meditation, ultimately leads to the result of being less attached to outcomes, which, by the way, is the only way I know of to arrive at deep inner peace. Nonattachment is not a new idea and was espoused by the Buddha more than 2,300 years ago.

How does meditation contribute to nonattachment? When we go deep into the meditative state, we can encounter the realm of nonduality. With regular meditation, this state becomes as real or even more real than the realm of duality or the physical plane. As the mystics have described through the ages—and is now corroborated by quantum physics—what we experience in the physical plane is an illusion based on our physical sense perception—a shadowy reflection of a truer reality that we can only glimpse in moments of deep meditation or mystical revelation. We are all pure energy, pure love, and all connected at the level of essence.

With the repetitive experience of nonduality, meditation helps us to recognize that no matter what happens on the physical plane, at the level of true reality, everything is perfect just the way it is. Energy cannot be destroyed—it only changes. Everything is infinite, including the essence of who we really are. When we look at our challenges from a larger, wider perspective, one aligned with true reality, we recognize that everything is unfolding for the purpose of our evolving consciousness, both individually and collectively, which leads to an ever-expanding experience of non-attachment, deep inner peace, and joyful living. Chapter 5, "Supporting Spiritual Practices," offers expanded information about radical gratitude, the joy factor, nonattachment, and other practices that lead to an ever-increasing life of peace, joy, and love.

INNER PEACE

Perhaps the most commonly sought-after benefit from meditation over time is inner peace. To quote Eckhart Tolle, "You find peace not by rearranging the circumstances of your life, but by realizing who you are at the deepest level." Meditation is the clearest and most effective way of achieving this result.

Inner peace means remaining emotionally calm inside, even when events of the world are chaotic and challenging. So how does meditation contribute to such a state? With consistent and continued practice, the deep peace that can be experienced in meditation familiarizes us with this state. The more we experience it inwardly during our quiet time, the more we are inspired and motivated to experience it in our lives throughout our daily activities.

In a way, meditation grooms us for what is truly important in life. As we attune ourselves to the inner experiences of deep peace, unconditional love, radiant light, and oneness, there is an increased desire to live life from the presence of these qualities. This doesn't mean such a practice will always be easy. We can affirm an intention to be at peace, continually practice it, and still get thrown off-center when challenges emerge. The practice previously mentioned of looking for the magic in every experience can help this, which can lead to nonjudgment and, ultimately, to enlightenment.

SPIRITUAL UNDERSTANDING AND MYSTICAL EXPERIENCE

Most meditation practices, especially those from Eastern philosophy, and New Age and New Thought in the West, emphasize that we are not separate from Infinite Source, God, Higher Power, Tao, Spirit, or whatever name one wants to give to It. In fact, I find complete agreement even with atheists on this matter. When I ask an atheist if he or she believes there is a creative force in the universe, the answer I most always receive is yes. This is our point of agreement. A spiritual or religious person will agree that God is a Creative Force. At a basic level then, we are all talking about the same thing. Meditation can lead one to deeper spiritual or even mystical experience regardless of one's religious affiliation or whether one even considers the state of oneness as spiritual.

From the philosophy of the ancient Greeks, pantheism is the expression of God immanent—God existing equally in all creation. It seems interesting to me that there are so many religious arguments about what God is. If God is infinite and all things, then there is no description of God that is not true. As I point out in *The Magic of the Soul*, the only time we get off track is when we try to delineate what God isn't, since God, or whatever name we ascribe, is everything. Every religion is either based in mysticism, such as Buddhism, Taoism, and Hinduism to a large extent, or has a mystical branch, like Kabbalah in Judaism, Gnosticism in Christianity, and Sufism in Islam. The mystical philosophical systems all say essentially the same thing: God is in everything, and the only way to experience God fully is through deep introspection, meditation, and mystical experience.

I interviewed Swami Satchidananda for *Meditation Magazine* in 1987. He was quite involved in interfaith work in addition to his role as a world-famous teacher of meditation and Hinduism. In the article I entitled "The Many Roads Home," he said this: "Once I was at the Vatican talking to a cardinal who questioned me, 'How can there be many paths to the same goal, God?' I said, 'Sir, you are living in Rome, so you of all people should understand. All roads lead to Rome! If Rome itself can have so many roads, why do we think that our home will have only one road?' So, we have to accept others' approaches to God."[9] The deeper one goes in one's spiritual path through meditation, prayer, or other spiritual practice, the less the focus tends to be on differences and mental constructs of God, and the more the heart understanding and experience of God unfolds as a presence of pure energy, light, love, and creative expression.

If everything that exists is an expression of God, then we must be as well. Meditation leads us to this ultimate realization. I acknowledge, of course, some philosophies that embrace meditation may believe in an anthropomorphic God and others, such as Buddhism, may not believe in a supreme being at all. Yet there is a realization of Buddha consciousness that a Buddhist is moving toward. In Christianity, there is one God, but also the Holy Spirit (in most Christian denominations), an aspect of the one God potentially manifest in humankind and nature. Atheists may achieve a deeper understanding of purpose and unity as human beings. To me and most who have advanced down the meditative path to mystical experience, it's all the same, just different names, like the song written by Daniel Nahmod, "One Power."[10] The chorus of the song sums it up perfectly:

> *Call it God, call it Spirit*
> *Call it Jesus, call it Lord*
> *Call it Buddha, Ba'ha'ulla*
> *Angel's Wings or Heaven's Door*
> *But whatever name you give it*
> *It's all One Power, can't you see?*
> *It's the power of the love in you and me.*

ENLIGHTENMENT

Many meditation practices, especially in Eastern traditions, hold the promise of enlightenment. One definition I like on this subject is the following: "The enlightened being is one who sees enlightenment (or at the very least, the potential of enlightenment) everywhere he or she looks." If I look at a situation, an individual, the world, and see mostly problems, then I am living in the realm of problems and most likely worry a good deal of my time. If I recognize that the situation, individual, and the world is on a journey of enlightenment and that everyone and everything is in the perfect place on that journey, then I am living in the realm of solution. Then I am at peace. Then I have a greater ability to create positive change. The level of peace we feel inside is perfectly proportionate to our ability to manifest what we want to see.

I believe that enlightenment, like everything else in life, is relative. One person may seem enlightened to some, and that same person may consider others more enlightened than him- or herself. Many who have been considered enlightened have had situations that would demonstrate otherwise. In my estimation and experience, anyone who is in physical form continues to have some degree of human challenge or relative imperfection. Embracing challenge and imperfection leads to higher levels of inner peace, joy, love, and enlightenment.

For an article in *Meditation Magazine*, I had the opportunity to interview Pir Vilayat Inayat Khan, the leader of the Sufi movement in the West at the time (and the son of the Sufi master Hazrat Inayat Khan), who was in my opinion one of the most enlightened beings I've ever met. Understanding that Sufism is an integrated spiritual philosophy, I asked him about how we deal with human emotion. Paraphrasing, his answer was essentially that anger is healthy as long as it is harnessed in a way that creates positive change. As far as pain and suffering, it's okay to have pain and to suffer, and one can still be happy (I would call it joyful) at the same time. And fear is also healthy: "If not for fear, we'd be doing more stupid things than we're doing now."[11]

Enlightenment, like every path or goal, is not about the destination but the journey. We are all enlightened as far as the truth of who we really are. We are all on a journey to realizing our essential truth, and wherever we are on that journey is absolutely the perfect place to be. When we go deep into meditation, quiet the mind, dissolve duality, experience the infinite joy, love, bliss, and oneness of all life, we are enlightened in that moment. You can stop reading for a moment, go into this state, and then for this moment . . . you are enlightened. Try it now, or jump to Meditation Practice, chapter 4. Or keep reading and wait for another moment—whatever brings you the most joy, my beloved reader.

In the moments and periods of time I have experienced what I would call enlightenment, I have found that being enlightened is not about being devoid of human emotions and experiences, such as pain, fear, or even righteous anger. It's really about how we perceive and/or frame our human experience.

When I can see the beauty in my own pain or the pain of

another, then I am enlightened. In fact, when I embrace my pain and go deep into it, what I find is my deepest love. I couldn't feel pain if there wasn't something or someone I love at the heart of it. When people share with me that they have lost a loved one, spouse, mother, or father, I will usually say something like, "I know the sadness you feel, the tears you are crying, are a beautiful testimony to your love for this individual." This, of course, does not take away the pain, but it helps the individual to focus not just on the pain, but more fully on the love. The only way pain heals is to be introduced to love.

When I see the beauty in my fear or the fear of another, I am enlightened. When I embrace my fear and go deep into it, what I find is my deepest sensitivity and compassion. In assisting people in embracing and loving their own fear, I have found that what is then integrated are the common aspects of the inner child: sensitivity, playfulness, and creativity.

When I see the beauty in my anger or the anger of another, I am enlightened. When I embrace my anger and go deep into it, what I find are my deepest values. Anger is most often the result of the experience of some value not being honored. Naturally, these emotions may not appear as their deeper expressions if we don't go deep. When we resist or judge them, they remain unconscious and play out in ways that are uncomfortable or damaging. When we go deep, when we are mindful, when we love and accept them, we uncover the beauty.

As a practice toward enlightenment, we can ask, "What is the magic in any situation? What is the greater freedom, joy, or love that wants to emerge from a situation?" And when I find it difficult to do so because I am in an experience of pain, fear, anger, or any uncomfortable feeling, I can ask, "What is the magic, joy, love, and power within my feelings?"

{ 3 }

GETTING STARTED

You can meditate nearly anywhere, but most people who meditate like to find a comfortable spot in their home, or outside when the weather is nice, where it is quiet with pleasant surroundings. Many create an altar with various items that invoke a sense of calm or spiritual presence that they can gaze at before they close their eyes for meditation or continue to gaze at if it is an opened-eye meditation. Meditating in the same spot on a daily basis accumulatively builds up a frequency of energy that helps to deepen the meditative practice over time.

MEDITATION TOOLS

As far as meditation tools, some suggestions are listed here, and you can find specific examples and where to find them in the resources section:

- Incense (frankincense and sandalwood are my favorites, and patchouli is quite nice as well), sage, sweetgrass, palo santo (a sweet-smelling wood with reported healing properties from the Amazon), essential oils, or other fragrances can be used to stimulate a calming olfactory experience. You can find incense in various forms, including sticks, oils, gums, resins, cones, and powders. There are also various products for burning them, including holders for sticks, pots for resins, gums, holders and plates for cones, and burners for oils.

- Candles can be lit and gazed at before, after, and/or during the session. You can find candles with most scents that are available in incense form, or unscented if you prefer. Burning one or more candles at a time can be done as personal preference dictates.

- Soft meditation or New Age music, nature sounds, or guided meditation apps can augment the meditative experience. Insight Timer is a phone/computer app that has thousands of guided meditations and musical selections. Please see additional suggestions in the resources section under "products." Another effective auditory stimulus is to ring a bell (Tibetan bowls work well for this), and as the sound trails off, drift into meditation and allow the fading sound to pull your consciousness outward with it, expanding into peace and bliss.

- Mind machines that provide goggles and headphones to transmit light and sound signals have been available for decades to help produce alpha and theta brain waves. These machines can be especially helpful for beginners.

- Mandalas can be gazed into as a visual stimulus that can lead one into altered states of consciousness. You can find original mandala art, prints, and tapestries to beautify your home that can also be used as meditation tools.

- Crystals and other minerals are believed to radiate specific energies for healing and mood enhancement. These as well as many others are recommended to support your meditation experience: clear quartz, amethyst, rose quartz, citrine, black tourmaline, carnelian, and aventurine. Fountains can add calming ambiance to your meditative space. You can find beautiful tabletop fountains for your altar or any space near your meditation spot.

POSTURE

Sitting cross-legged in lotus position on the floor, a mat, or a cushion is a classic Eastern position, but certainly not required. Many in the Western world prefer to sit in a chair for greater comfort with sitting meditation. There is no right or wrong position, but it is highly recommended to sit with a straight back so that the energy can flow easily up the spine, balancing the chakras—the seven energy centers within our energy body that move from the bottom of the spine to the top of the head.

Lying down is an option and is obviously advantageous if one is using meditation in preparation for relaxation or sleep. If you want to achieve a poised yet present state without lots of racing thoughts and without falling asleep, then sitting erect is advised. Depending on the chair I'm sitting in, I like to sit with my back away from the backrest or at least have a pillow behind my lower back so my spine is easily in a straight position with my head supported by my neck rather than resting on a headrest. One benefit to this posture is if you do start to fall asleep, your body will let you know when your head falls forward and automatically bounces back to protect your neck.

What is most important is to be comfortable. If you are meditating for a longer period of time, like twenty minutes or more, feel free to move your head to stretch your neck or other part of your body as well. If we can meditate while walking, dancing, or playing a sport, surely we can stay in meditation while moving the body to maintain comfort. There are those who teach remaining perfectly still as an important component to meditation and that the meditator eventually can transcend any and all discomfort, no matter how long they remain in one position. In my experience, it is far better to be comfortable.

I attended a group meditation meeting in my early twenties in a room with very creaky wooden chairs. It was a completely silent meditation with no guiding whatsoever, which I do prefer and enjoy. At first there were a few creaking sounds from the chairs, then more, until the room was filled with creaking chair noises. The leader proclaimed in a gruff voice, "If we cannot be still, then we cannot meditate." Not my type of meditation—too rigid!

What to do with the hands? The simplest and probably most common hand position is palms facing up and resting on the thighs. Hands down is fine, too. It is recommended that legs and hands not be crossed to remain open physically, which is symbolic of being open emotionally, mentally, and spiritually. Beginning with the conventional wisdom is a good idea to fully experience the benefits that have been time-tested, but ultimately, I recommend you find your own comfort zone and create your own conventional wisdom based on your experience.

A traditional pose involves palms up, with forefinger and thumb pressed lightly together. This mudra, or sacred hand position, is symbolic. The index finger is symbolic of our personal will. We use it to point things out or point at a person (even though it has been deemed "impolite") when we want to get an important idea across. Our thumb is symbolic of universal will. Thumbs-up means "good job, something positive is happening." So symbolically, we are bringing together personal will with universal will. We also create a circuit of energy by creating a circle with our finger and thumb in this position.

HELPFUL HINTS

- Prepare your space so it is calm and tranquil. It is recommended that you normally meditate in the same spot in your home to easily and comfortably slip into your meditative journey.

- Turn off your phone.

- Tell others in your environment that you are having quiet time and to please not disturb.

- Make sure the temperature is comfortable.

- Be sure and visit the bathroom if applicable before beginning so your physical comfort will be maintained.

- Some people find it helpful to keep a journal close by. If you have pressing thoughts come up in meditation and don't want to forget them, you can open your eyes, write them down, and return to meditation with a freer mind.

- Set a timer if you have a prescribed amount of time that you want to meditate, so you don't have to be checking or thinking about the time.

THINGS TO REMEMBER

Expect it to be easy. Meditation in many ways is a metaphor for life. If we expect everything to be easy, whatever task ahead of us will most definitely be easier than if we expect it to be difficult. In my twenties, I was very tied into the expectation that projects or goals would be difficult, especially if I did not yet know the how of it. I had an epiphany and recognized how much struggle I had created as a result of my belief. From then on, anytime I noticed myself expecting something to be difficult (and it was the discomfort of the thought that became the cue), I would simply turn it around and expect the task or goal to be an absolute breeze. I never looked back and life has continued to get easier and easier over the past forty years.

Why is it the most difficult thing to do as a human being is . . . nothing, being still and quiet of mind . . . when all that's really required is surrender? Meditation could also be defined as "a process of surrender—surrendering the control of the personal self or ego and control of the analytical mind to a higher expression and vibration of energy." There are times when I may be experiencing some degree of stress in my life, and as I go into meditation, I consider it such a relief to surrender any concerns of the personality and simply let it all go to experience the "other self"— the timeless higher, freer expression of myself as pure peace, love, light, and bliss. Gangaji, a North American spiritual teacher, says, "Be still. It takes no effort to be still; it is utterly simple. When your mind is still, you have no name, you have no past, you have no relationships, you have no country, you have no spiritual attainment, you have no lack of spiritual attainment. There is just the presence of beingness with itself."

What makes anything difficult? Isn't it simply that we are not accomplishing the task at the level that we want to? Certainly, there is value to striving for excellence, but if we judge that we are failing if we don't reach our goal, then life will be filled with much disappointment. I recently asked a client if they were the only person in the world who played guitar, how they would judge their skill level. You'd be the best! If it's all about the journey, as we hear over and over, then let's chuck the judgment and have fun with whatever we are doing and at whatever level of skill we are doing it while we stretch for higher levels of excellence in a non-judgmental and joyful way.

And what happens when we can truly let go of control? Only then can we be totally free. In retreats I have offered in various locations in California, including Catalina Island, and Saskatch-ewan and Alberta, Canada, I usually include a trust fall. When you are standing on a table or a rock with seven or more people behind you encouraging you to let go and trust to fall backward into their arms, fear inevitably comes up—not rational fear, of course. Intellectually, I know my friends will catch me. It's the emotional fear of letting go of control that creates the hesitancy. I've had people stand there for ten minutes or more before finally letting go. I always experience a huge rush when I let go and fall backward.

This morning in my meditation, I noticed the correlation between that trust-fall rush and letting go of the control of the mind and ego during deep meditation. What I experience is a profound expansiveness. Once I let go completely, I am no longer me. I become one with all that is, not only conceptually, but energetically. My entire "beingness" is no longer contained within the personality named Patrick Harbula. I am no longer any-thing; I have become everything. During a recent meditation training in Edmonton,

Canada, someone said to me they experienced nothing and continued to say, "When you realize nothing, you have everything."

The inner peace that comes from meditation and continues to expand over time is the motivating factor for continuing to practice for those who can appreciate the importance of this profound benefit. Tibetan Buddhist monk Geshe Kelsang Gyatso says, "When we understand clearly that inner peace is the real source of happiness, and how, through spiritual practice, we can experience progressively deeper levels of inner peace, we will develop tremendous enthusiasm to practice."

Make it fun. There was a time in my life when I practiced meditation as a discipline. What has evolved for me in the area of meditative practice, as well as virtually every other aspect of living, is to meditate for the joy of it rather than as a discipline or because I think I have to or should. From my ongoing experience, I find that whatever I do for the joy of doing it is always more beneficial than forcing myself to participate in that same activity. How I define joy, by the way, is not the opposite of sadness—that's happiness, which is a quality more aligned with the personal self. *Joy* to me is a pervasive spiritual quality that can be present, even in moments of pain, loss, or sadness and is synonymous with deep inner peace and connection.

The spiritual joy of which I am writing is also a lasting joy. It's not simply being happy and certainly not about instant gratification. By virtue of being a spiritual or soul quality, it is by nature long-term. To determine if what I am choosing to do for spiritual joy is effective, I can ask, "How will I feel a month from now if I choose to participate in a particular activity or go in a particular direction?" The answer becomes a compass for joyful living, and, by the way, the most powerful demonstration of self-love we can offer ourselves is to do what brings us joy.

In relation to meditation, what this means is rather than

thinking, "I must sit down and meditate today and then another six days this week," I can ask myself, "Will sitting down today and another six days this week bring me lasting joy? Looking back a month or two from now, will it bring me more joy to meditate or not to meditate today?" Perhaps the answer will be that four or five days will bring more joy, because there will be more spaciousness around the practice.

Sometimes the answer may be that it will not bring me the most joy today, because I've got a ton of things to do, and it will put more stress on myself to spend twenty minutes meditating than if I attend to the things that I want to accomplish. Of course, in this case, I could modify the question to "Will it bring me more lasting joy if I meditate for three minutes today than if I don't at all?" Perhaps one could argue that such a practice is a form of discipline and that we're just talking semantics. My encouragement, however, is to find a way to make your practice light. If it feels forced, you're probably not going to continue your practice very long, and your benefits will not be as great. If you find that every day you're too busy, then that's an indication that a major shift may be in order. Is it bringing you lasting joy to be so busy that you don't have time to take part in the activities that will bring you lasting joy, balance, and wholeness?

Make it consistent. It is far better to have a shorter consistent practice than more sporadic longer sessions of practice. For example, meditating ten minutes per day, five days a week will bring more noticeable and lasting results than meditating once a week for two hours, even though two hours is more than double the total amount of time spent meditating per week.

When I was in my early twenties, I had a lot of negative, unhealed emotions and energy, which led me to the study and practice of transpersonal psychology in my later twenties. The techniques from transpersonal psychology had a profound effect on my healing and integration. Before I found those techniques, many of which are meditative in nature, I used more traditional meditation to heal. Because the negativity was so strong and persistent, I would meditate three or more times each day, simply surrendering to light and love. This practice was an excellent beginning solution to my ongoing healing and integration.

Commit to your practice. Make your commitment inviting and exceedable (my word). This is the formula I use with clients and students that applies to all types of action steps, including meditation. I make a distinction between goals and actions. If you want to meditate twenty minutes per day, seven days a week, make that your goal. Your action step, which you commit to at 100 percent (you may not always achieve 100 percent, but that is the intention), could be to meditate a minimum of ten minutes per day, four days per week. Then, if you do twenty minutes for some of those days and/or five or six days a week, you are exceeding your commitment. How much better will it feel to exceed your intention than to just meet it or fall short? When most people make a commitment to every day, once they miss the first day, they feel like they have failed and often give up completely shortly afterward.

On the other hand, there can be a benefit to an everyday commitment for any amount of time (say, for twenty-one days, for example) if you are able to follow through or even if you do miss a day or more. If you don't complete the commitment, don't judge yourself. Instead, start over and recommit to your intention. Even if you never complete the twenty-one days, you will more than likely end up meditating more than you would with a four-day-a-week practice. Just make sure that whatever the commitment, you are continuing to do your practice for the joy of doing it rather than because you feel you have to or should.

Get support. Avail yourself to meditation groups, classes, and/

or a meditation coach. It helps to meditate in groups, especially if they have experienced meditators. You can find classes and coaches or trainers from many different sources and styles in the meditation resources section at the end of this book.

Get a meditation buddy. Find a friend who will be an accountability partner with you. You can check in daily or weekly by phone, text, email, messaging, etc. You can support each other in your practices and share what is working as far as meditation styles and forms as well as your challenges.

Surrender to a higher power. Here's a tip that I find really helps make meditation easy: as you are meditating, focus on the benefits of nonthinking. We have all of our waking consciousness to use our mind in active or even overactive ways. I find that I can allow my dissatisfaction or discontent with the constant buzzing of monkey mind to inspire me to just give it up and surrender.

To take this a step further in effortlessness, surrender the busy mind to a higher power. Rather than *trying* to be at peace, consider allowing a benevolent higher power—spiritual guides, masters, inner guru, a specific enlightened being, the Buddha, the Christ, angels, Spirit, and/or God—to guide you into pure bliss, peace, love, and light. Allow Spirit to take you on a journey that may go to places in consciousness that you don't even know exist.

Expect that you will go deeper. Recently I tried a new meditation practice. By the way, another tip for becoming a meditator is to write a book on it. This project is bringing me incredible joy and has definitely upped my intention to go deeper in meditation. This new technique is to expect and intend that as I go into still mind, I will progressively go deeper and enjoy a more expanded consciousness with each passing second.

What I often find is that when I get to still mind and I am completely free of control, my thoughts sneak in through the open door. What starts with a simple thought like "I can share this experience in my writing today" trails off into thinking about writing the next section of the book, then off to thinking about how I can use this technique in my next class. Then I realize I'm thinking again, invite the thought in without any resistance, and again affirm that with each passing second, I will effortlessly go deeper. I like to play with tricking my own mind as well. I often experiment with assuming that any thoughts coming in are actually fuel for still mind. As I watch them go by and/or invite them in, they are actually fueling the deepening.

Invite "distractions" to be part of the bliss. In teaching meditation locally as well as across the continent in workshops, I have found that the most helpful hint I offer people is rather than resisting thoughts, feelings, or sensations, simply invite them into the meditation. A common strategy is to simply watch these experiences as they arise, and in mindfulness meditation, this is the general purpose, to simply be more mindful of whatever we are experiencing in the moment.

For example, one can watch the thoughts as they go by, like watching the boxcars on a train go by. What I find even more helpful is to let the thoughts, feelings, or sensations become part of the meditation. In doing so, they tend to dissolve into the blissful experience. I assume that any thought coming into play is doing so because it wants to become part of the bliss. It wants to become enlightened; it wants to meditate with me. Again, as a perfect metaphor for life, whatever we resist persists and, in fact, magnifies. Anything we embrace and accept subsides and ultimately transforms and integrates.

This applies to feelings and sensations as well. If we resist a particular feeling that we don't like whether in meditation or not, it will continue to bug us. By inviting the feeling into the bliss and welcoming it, it will easily dissolve into the meditative experience. In life, this is true as well. In working with individuals as a coach, one of the most important exercises I offer is to help people love and accept every aspect of themselves. We cannot love ourselves any more than we love the parts of ourselves that we love the least. My simple metaphor for this is to imagine that any feeling or behavior that you may judge as negative is a young child that you are responsible for and is showing up as that particular behavior or feeling. I often hear teachers say that we have to embrace our shadow (the unhealed aspect of self) and in the next sentence say we have to get over our fears so we can accomplish our goals.

If you told a fearful child "I have to get over you, or set you aside," how would it feel for the child and how would the child likely react? He or she would become more fearful and perhaps even throw a tantrum. Every part of us and every unhealed emotion and limiting thought is simply trying to get acceptance and love. By loving these aspects of self, they become healed and we become integrated and whole.

The same is true for physical discomforts or pain. When we resist pain and judge it as bad or negative, it persists and magnifies. When we embrace and love our physical discomforts, they relax and become less painful and ultimately improve, because love is the most powerful healing force there is. In a microcosmic way, this dynamic all works out in the meditative process, by loving, accepting, and embracing whatever comes into awareness.

The same is true for noises or sounds in meditation. Our experience is determined to a large degree by what we name things. During a meditation workshop in Calgary, Canada, at the home of a good friend, one person came out of a fifty-minute meditation and announced that the "ticking of that clock was disturbing my peace." Another participant described the ticking as "a steady metronome bringing me deeper and deeper." Everything is to us what we name it to be.

During another class I was teaching on meditation, I addressed the strategy of using "distracting" sounds as a call to go deeper. The next day, I had the opportunity to practice what I preach in a big way—as usual, I sat down to meditate in my meditation chair to the right of my altar when I heard the loudest sustained noise I'd ever heard in my home. We were doing some remodeling, and the workers were drilling through pipes in the bathroom adjacent to the master bedroom in which I was sitting. Rather than judge the sound as a distraction, I used it as a calling to go deeper. It was one of the deepest meditations I've ever experienced. The Absolute, which we experience in deep stillness, is in everything, including the drill, the driller, the sound, the music in the other room, someone yelling outside, and, of course, every thought, feeling, and sensation we can possibly have. Once reframed, the "distractions" can become our allies in the deepening.

Slip into the GAP. Many authors and meditation trainers speak about "the gap," the space between thoughts. A good friend of mine, Reverend Steve Rambo, uses this as an acronym for the God Awareness Place. The point here is to once again observe the thoughts and then find the gap between them. As we exercise the meditation muscle, the gap can become wider and the thoughts fewer and further between. We will practice all the tips above and various meditation styles in chapter 4: "Meditation Practice."

Allow whatever is to be. It is important with meditation and any spiritual practice to be mindful about not using it as a means of escape, what is often called a "spiritual bypass." If we meditate, say affirmations, pray, or visualize to improve our lives or simply feel better, and at the end of it, we still have a knot in our gut; this is our body and emotions telling us that it needs a deeper or more cathartic release. Otherwise we may be inadvertently repressing emotions, which is never a healthy strategy. There are many methods of releasing and healing uncomfortable feelings, including journaling, crying, screaming (into a pillow if needed), punching a pillow, working out. In chapter 5, "Supporting Spiritual Practices," I outline a practice I developed for ongoing and consistent emotional release and healing called "shift and release."

A very simple practice I use when it's called for is to release emotion at the beginning of my meditation. If I feel an emotional discomfort and/or tension in my body, I tune in to it and allow whatever sound that wants to emerge to come out—sometimes tears or sobbing, shuddering, or even screaming. While this was a more common strategy earlier in my practice, I find it necessary only rarely, as years of healing have led me to a place of inner peace, but I still find it valuable on the rare occasions when discomfort is present.

If I sit down to meditate and my consciousness or psyche is half-filled with pain, fear, or anger, then it is unlikely that I will be able to go very deep into meditation. Once I completely void myself of the uncomfortable feelings in a loving and self-accepting way, then I become an empty vessel that can be filled 100 percent with spiritual light, love, and peace.

Accept and love yourself along your spiritual path. In one of my workshops I ask this question, and I will ask it now of you, my beloved reader: "What would your life be like if it were 100 percent free of critical self-judgment?" Previously, I had said "all judgment" and then remembered self-judgment is really the only kind of judgment there is. If I'm judging another, it means that I am projecting something I judge as negative about myself onto another. I'm sure your answer is something like, "I'd be free, empowered, joyful."

I've had people tell me that they were actually less self-critical before they began a spiritual path—when they were "clueless." Once we are on a spiritual path, we now have an ideal that we are moving toward, and we tend to judge ourselves in comparison to that ideal. We forget to notice and appreciate how far we've come. It is just as important, if not more important, to accept yourself as you are.

Appreciate and honor exactly where you are on your path. As John Lennon and Paul McCartney wrote in "All You Need Is Love," "There's nowhere you can be that isn't where you were meant to be." And one of my favorite and truest quotes is from Carl Rogers, the founder of humanistic psychology: "The curious paradox is that when I accept myself as I am, then I change." As long as I'm judging myself, I am keeping myself stuck. My baseline spiritual practice is to accept and love myself as I am in all my humanness, *no matter what.*

A question I ask many of my clients is "On a scale of one to ten, how much do you love yourself?" If it's less than a ten, then there is room for improvement. If it's less than a five, then this is the most important focus of your life. One way to assess the answer to this question is to ask how loving and encouraging your inner dialogue is on a regular basis. When you make a mistake, do you hear in your head something like "You idiot!" Or do you hear "It's okay, this is part of being human," or "I love myself, no matter what"?

While on your meditative and spiritual path, make loving and accepting yourself no matter what a priority in every situation. Simply put, give yourself a break—you deserve it! We're all on a path to ever-increasing expressions of love, and we are all in our absolutely perfect place on that journey.

WHAT TO EXPECT

It is likely, unless you are already the most enlightened being in history, that you will experience sensations, feelings, and especially thoughts—sometimes even racing thoughts—that come up when you begin your meditation practice and, as a matter of fact, you will continue to experience this to some degree (less as time goes by) throughout your journey as a meditator. As stated, all this is part of the process, and it is best not to judge yourself for whatever level of success you are experiencing. Remember that, like anything else, the more you practice, the easier it becomes. It is just like exercising a muscle. The more you exercise it, the stronger it gets, and the stronger your practice will become over time. Deepak Chopra advises, "Meditation is not a way of making your mind quiet. It is a way of entering into the quiet that is already there—buried under the fifty thousand thoughts the average person thinks every day."

One dynamic that I experienced early in my practice and which has been reported by many of the students in my trainings is a fear that can come up while slipping into very deep levels of consciousness. What happens when the mind becomes completely still is that we can actually lose sense of who we are at the level of personality. When we begin to merge in consciousness into mystical states, it can literally feel like we are dying, and our instinct for self-preservation kicks in and brings us back to personal identification. If this happens for you, recognize it as a wonderful step in your progress. It means you are quieting the mind to the point of entering pure bliss and oneness. As you continue to move into still mind, the fear or self-preservation reflex will gradually subside as a result of realizing that you didn't actually die in the moments of shifting identification from the personal self to the transpersonal or soul self, connected with all other life in the mystical experience of pure bliss.

On the other side of the consciousness coin from monkey mind is unconsciousness. You may just fall asleep during meditation. It has been said that the ideal state of mind for meditation is poised yet alert. I like the word "present" better than "alert," though. "Alert" feels a little too intense. Remaining in a surrendered, peaceful yet present state is really the journey of the meditation practice and exercising your meditation muscle. If you find yourself dozing off, don't be concerned. You will ultimately train your mind to remain present. As mentioned, sitting up straight will help the training process. Meditating when you are fresh and rested is also important and is why most people like to meditate in the morning shortly after arising from sleep. By meditating first thing in the morning, your mind is also free from distractions that arise from daily activities. Once I check email or social media, I've got a flourishing of new thoughts to dance around in my meditative space, so I almost always meditate first thing after brushing my teeth.

Since we're expecting it to be easy, you may find yourself slipping easily and effortlessly into deep mindfulness and/or still yet present mind. In this state, you may have mystical experiences, a feeling or sense of deep connectedness or oneness with all life. You may go beyond time and space. You may find your personal identity dissolving into the mystery. You may hear a voice spoken to you or spoken as you. You may see images: pure white light, radiant golden light, or other visions that are completely unique to your own experience.

About ten years into my practice, when I would go really deep, the image of a golden radiant being would spontaneously emerge, and I would be with that image in a state of stillness. The being looked much like the East Indian god Ganesh. I don't know for sure if I had seen the image before, and I certainly didn't know anything about Ganesh at the time.

You may receive messages in deep meditation. Some of the thoughts that come to me in deep mindfulness and slipping in and out of still mind are profound. This is a good thing and why inviting thoughts in is helpful. A couple of years ago, I was meditating while camping on Catalina Island in California. The message that came to me was not a completely new idea, but it was a clearer understanding of what I already knew: Spirit, God, the Infinite Universe delights in expressing through every human experience, including love, hatred, creativity, fear, joy, sadness, hope, anger, compassion, rage, acceptance, discontentment, caring, abuse, righteousness, oppression, tenderness, violence, peace, and war.

I realize this may not make perfect sense to everyone. What I have experienced, as have mystics down through the ages, is that at the level of nonduality, everything is perfect. All human experience leads to the evolution of consciousness. All human experience leads to a higher expression of love. Even the most violent act is a call for love.

You may experience no sights or sound but simply feel yourself as one with all life, as pure radiance, love, and peace. Oftentimes in my meditations during the past ten years or so, I feel my energy body expanding until I am the energy of all life. I actually kinesthetically, physically feel myself as one with all that is.

The following is a passage from *The Magic of the Soul*, written eighteen years ago, illustrating a profound meditative experience:

Today in my morning meditation, I reached a level of peace so profound I didn't want to leave it. I felt that the energy that I am beyond my self-identity was more real, more solid than how I experience myself in physical form. I was completely connected—no, more than connected—I was one in that moment with the energy of all life. Tears streamed down my face (as they are now while I write these words and re-experience the sensation) because the experience was filled with such beauty. But they were not "my" tears. They were the tears of all life flowing through a particular identification known as Patrick. I experienced my personality, or the personality of Patrick, as one aspect of that one life, no more or less important (and just as beautiful) in that moment than the grass it sat on, the trees surrounding it, or the wind flowing through and around it.[1]

What I have found in my trainings is that people experience meditation similar to the way they experience life. A person who processes information predominantly visually, for example, will have more of a visual experience in meditation. The person who is more auditory will experience the stillness as a sound, tone, voice, or humming. The kinesthetic individual will most likely *feel* the energy, the peace, the pure love, and the bliss. You may have some degree of all these experiences.

You may also experience nothing! Perhaps that is the greatest gift of all, to be lost in the void of complete nonexistence. No matter how you experience meditation, whether it's in the chattering of the mind, the cycling in and out of still mind, or the various ways you slip into mystical awareness, know that what you are experiencing is perfect for you at this particular time and your experience will expand and deepen as you continue down this path.

{ 4 }

MEDITATION PRACTICE

Let's begin actually meditating. You can use the following meditations to get started on your meditation path or to add new techniques and styles to your existing practice. You can read these meditations into your own recording device and listen to them said in your own voice.

The first session, entitled "Meditation Sampler," is precisely the format I use in my meditation workshops. It is a longer form offering many different styles and techniques in one extended session. I usually lead these for about forty minutes to an hour or so. Virtually everyone experiences them as feeling much shorter. At the end, I sometimes ask how long people thought we were in meditation. The answers usually vary, ranging from ten to twenty minutes.

I used to be hesitant about leading long meditations, especially with newbies. Then I remembered that I became really good at meditating by participating in group meditations called "transmission meditation," which involved sitting with a group of people in complete silence for about three hours at a time, holding our attention at the level of the third eye (the point slightly above and at the center of the brows), and allowing our group to be a transmitter of light, love, and power as a service to the planet and all sentient beings. Sitting for long periods in meditation will definitely build the meditation muscle.

In the following Meditation Sampler, I offer a specific style or technique, then allow silence to practice it. I then introduce another style or technique, allow more silence, and so on. As I say in my trainings, feel free to completely ignore a specific technique, or my voice if you are listening, and continue with whatever technique you find most helpful. Feel free to use all these techniques together in one long session, or simply use those you like the best individually.

The last practice in the Meditation Sampler is an invitation to sing a simple but powerful Sanskrit chant. I find that if no other practice helps to calm and still the mind, Vedic chanting does the trick for most people. The words are "Ram Jai, Jai Ram, Jai Jai Ram Om." In some Vedic traditions, Ram (pronounced "rom," rhyming with "mom") means "Supreme Being." Jai (pronounced "jay," rhyming with "hay") means "praise." Om (pronounced "om," rhyming with "home") has many meanings, including "God" or "First Cause," and is a most sacred syllable used at the beginning and/or end of sacred chants, much like "Amen" is used at the end of a Christian prayer. In singing this song, we are praising and opening our hearts fully to Supreme Being or Creator in whatever form we understand It to be. You can also find many examples of simple Sanskrit chants on YouTube.

The seven meditations, beginning with Color Cycle on page 84, are guided meditations designed to take you into a deep meditative state. Spend several minutes in the deep meditation beyond the guiding portion and see if you can extend that time as your practice continues to evolve.

MEDITATION SAMPLER

Make sure that you are ready to meditate. Remember to:

- Prepare your space so it is calm and tranquil.

- Turn off your phone.

- Tell others in your environment that you are having quiet time and to please not disturb.

- Make sure the temperature is comfortable.

- Before beginning visit the bathroom (if necessary) so your physical comfort will be maintained.

Take a nice deep breath and let out a big heartfelt sigh. Let's do that once more, and this time, let it all go. Continue to breathe deeply, filling your lungs completely and expelling the breath completely. Feel your pelvic area expanding with each in breath and contracting with each out breath. With every breath, feel yourself becoming more and more relaxed, centered, and at peace. . . .

Now return to normal breathing. In mindfulness meditation, just observe whatever you notice without judgment or analysis. Just watch. As thoughts, feelings, or sensations arise, simply observe them. If you get lost in a thought, then come back to your intention of observation and watch that process. If you hear sounds, don't resist them, just observe them. You might even find as you give up judgment that you see the beauty in whatever you are observing. Continue to simply observe anything and everything that presents itself to your awareness. . . .

(Allow five minutes of silence.)

One Zen technique is to refrain from isolating or resisting sounds and sights if eyes are open but include everything in the environment. Be aware of any and all sounds around you—a ticking clock, an air conditioner or heater, traffic, birds, or other animal sounds outside or around you. Any loud noises also can be embraced and become part of your meditation. Feel your awareness expanding to include more and more sounds, and as your awareness expands, sense the sounds are no longer outside your awareness but contained within. As your awareness continues to expand, the sounds you are conscious of move closer and closer to the center of your awareness. Be aware of the busyness and energy outside the circle of your hearing, your consciousness expanding to include the activities in your city, state or province, country, the entire planet, and even this wide range of experience is now at the center of your expansive state. If at any time during this meditation you hear noises that distract you, you can come back to this practice and sense them near the center of your expanded awareness. Continue in this expanded state in silence.

(Allow five minutes of silence.)

With silent mantra, simply choose a word or phrase that speaks to your divine truth or praises your understanding of divinity. A common Sanskrit mantra is "Om mani padme hum," which means "the jewel within the lotus" and symbolizes the opening of the lotus of the chakras, especially the heart, third eye, and crown chakras, to expose the jewel at its center. The fully opened lotus is a symbol of enlightenment. You can also choose an "I am" statement, such as "I am love, I am light, I am peace. I am That I Am" (identifying as the One Infinite Presence or God), or simply "I am." Another possibility is to focus on a sound or tone sounded internally, like the sacred Om. My favorite is a constant "ah" sound, sung with the voices of angels. Repeat the word, phrase, or sound over and over, not focusing on the meaning, but allowing the vibration to carry you to that sacred place of silence and communion with all life. . . .

(Allow five minutes of silence.)

Now breathe in through your nostrils and out through your mouth, creating a circle of breath. . . . In Watching-the-Breath Meditation, simply observe your breath as it travels in through your nose all the way down to the deepest point and out through your mouth on the exhale. Continue watching your breath. If thoughts, feelings, or sensations come to your attention, don't try to ignore or resist them. Invite them into the experience. Assume that any thought, feeling, sensation, or sound is coming forth because it wants to be part of the peace, love, light, and bliss that you are experiencing. Notice how easily these impressions dissolve into the peace when they are embraced. . . . (Allow about two minutes of silence.) Now observe the point between the in breath and out breath . . . and the point between the out breath and the in breath. These two points are the places of perfect balance between the pairs of opposites: the places of perfect balance between receiving and giving, positive and negative, yin and yang, light and dark, death and life, manifestation and dissolution, feminine and masculine, Spirit and matter, Mother Earth and Father Sky, Grandfather Sun and Grandmother Moon. . . . Continue to watch your breath and the points of perfect balance, wholeness, and oneness with all existence. . . .

(Allow five minutes of silence.)

I invite you to join in this breathing technique called Meditation for Stilling the Mind[1]. Take a deep breath and hold it.

Release your breath. Feel your awareness becoming lighter and lighter, lighter than the Earth of your body, lighter than the element of Earth. . . . Take another deep breath and hold it. Release your breath, and feel your awareness becoming still lighter, lighter than the water of your emotions, and lighter than the element of water. Take another deep breath and hold it. Release your breath, and feel your awareness becoming still lighter, lighter than the fires of your mind, and lighter than the element of fire. . . . Take another deep breath and hold it. Release your breath and feel your awareness becoming as light as the air of your soul, as light as the element of air. . . . Take another deep breath and hold it. Release your breath and feel your awareness becoming lighter even than the element of air, as light as the pure love of Spirit, as light as the Buddhic plane, the Atma, One Supreme Self. Remain in the pure light of Spirit, and if a sensation, feeling, or thought comes into play, take a deep breath and hold it, release, and feel your awareness once again becoming lighter than Earth, water, fire, and air.

(Allow five minutes of silence.)

I invite you to join in a visualization. Imagine that you are a point of light in infinite space in all directions. Nothing exists but you as this point of light. . . . Now see another point of light far off in the distance. Move your consciousness from your point of light to the second point of light, looking back at the first. . . . Now allow your consciousness to be in both points of light at the same time. . . . See a third point of light far off in the distance that creates a triangle between the now three points of light. Move your consciousness from the first two to the third point of light, looking back at the first two. Allow your consciousness to be in all three points of light at the same time. . . . Now see more points of light popping into existence inside the sphere of the triangle and outside the sphere as well. Allow your consciousness to be in all the points of light as they pop into being. See points of light populating the entire infinite and ever-expanding universe with each and every point filled with your consciousness, which is being stretched and expanded infinitely. Now see the points of light saturating the infinite space to the point that they are all connecting with one another until there is nothing left but infinite light that is your ever-expanding consciousness. Remain in the consciousness of ever-expanding light.

(Allow five minutes of silence.)

I invite you to join me in the following chant: "Ram Jai, Jai Ram, Jai Jai, Ram Om."

> *Ram Jai, Jai Ram, Jai Jai, Ram Om.*
> *Ram Jai, Jai Ram, Jai Jai, Ram Om.*
> *Ram Jai, Jai Ram, Jai Jai, Ram Om.*

Continue chanting for about five minutes or more. . . .
Now sing the chant softer.

> *Ram Jai, Jai Ram, Jai Jai, Ram Om.*

Softer still.

> *Ram Jai, Jai Ram, Jai Jai, Ram Om.*

As soft as you can.

> *Ram Jai, Jai Ram, Jai Jai, Ram Om.*

Whisper the words.

Ram Jai, Jai Ram, Jai Jai, Ram Om.

Now chant silently.

Ram Jai, Jai Ram, Jai Jai, Ram Om....

Continue as long as you like, and when you are ready, slowly and gently bring your awareness back to your surroundings. Feel the light, love, and peace you have accessed grounded in your body and through you deep down into Mother Earth. When it's right for you, bring your awareness back completely, take a nice deep breath, and open your eyes.

In a word, how do you feel?

DISIDENTIFICATION EXERCISE

Observe your body and sensations. *Where do you notice tension?*

Breathe deeply into those places. Notice how you can choose to relax your body. Observe the strength of your body. Recognize its incredible capacity to heal almost any illness. Do you know that nearly 97 percent of all illness can be healed by the body's natural processes? Notice how you can train and condition your body to do incredible feats if you choose to. Appreciate how your body responds to love and nurturing. Appreciate the magical construct of your body. Recognize that you can choose what kind of body you want by how you treat and condition it.

Affirm that you have a body and sensations and yet you are more than your body. *How do you choose to be in your body?*

Observe your feeling nature. Be aware of the different feelings you have experienced in this day. Notice how intense your emotions can be at times. Notice how powerful your love can be.

Let the love in your heart well up and overflow out of you in all directions. . . . Remember times when your feelings overwhelmed you. Think of times when you were able to direct your emotions skillfully. Recognize that you can choose how you wish to feel. Appreciate the magic in your feeling.

Affirm that you have feelings, yet you are more than your feelings. *How do you choose to live your feelings?*

Observe your thought nature. Appreciate how incredible the power of your mind is, how you can process and store large amounts of information, how you can think abstractly, how quickly your mind can shift from one thought to another, how it never stops even when you want it to, and how you can organize thoughts into belief systems. Be aware of the untapped regions of your mind. What exists in these regions? Recognize that no matter how strong your beliefs may be, you can choose to change them. You can choose how you want to think and the quality of the thoughts you entertain. How could you use your mind in more magical ways? How often does your mind wander in fantasy? Run wild in obsessive worry? How would you like your mind to be? How often is your mind still, open to receiving inspiration from above? How often is it engaged in creative expression? Be thankful for the magical qualities of thought and affirm that you have the ability to direct your mind and choose your beliefs.

Affirm that you have thoughts, yet you are more than your thoughts. *How do you choose to use your thoughts?*

Now ask yourself: If you are more than your body, mind, and emotions, who are you? Who is the observer, the one who chooses how to express your personality in this world? Identify with the center of yourself. Allow yourself to gently slip into the silence of the holy place that is your innermost soul.

MINDFULNESS BODY SCAN

The body scan meditation is usually done lying down on your back with palms up, but it can be done in any position, such as sitting in a chair or lying back on a recliner.

Once you are in position, observe your breathing. Watch the breath going in and out, breathing all the way in, filling your lungs, and feeling your abdomen expanding with each inhalation. Expel all the breath on the exhalation. Continue to breathe deeply and observe. Notice if there is any tension in your body; without judging, just notice and observe.

Now become aware of your feet. Appreciate how your feet have served you in helping you to get around, all the places your feet have taken you. Feel the sensation of your feet on the floor. Notice if there is tension or tightness in the muscles of your feet. Be aware of each toe on each foot. Notice the condition of each one. Be aware of the entire surface of the skin on your feet, as well as the insides of your feet, the veins and blood, the nerves, muscles, cells. As you breathe in, feel your breath going into your feet and toes. Notice if your feet are relaxing, loosening.

Allow your awareness to move up to your ankles. Are your ankles relaxed or is there some degree of tension? Be aware of the entire circumference of your ankles, the top, the bottom, and the sides, the skin, muscles, bones, and nerves within, the large Achilles tendon just above the heel. Breathe into your ankles and notice if they become even more relaxed.

Raise your attention to your calves. Become aware of the large muscles in the backs of your calves. Are they tense or relaxed? Once again observing without judgment, just watch. Observe the entire circumference of your calf, as well as the skin, muscles, tendons, blood flowing through your veins, bones, tibia, and fibula. Breathe into your calves and notice if they become even more relaxed.

Allow your awareness to move up to your knees. Is there any tension or pain within these precious joints that allow you to move, walk, and run? Appreciate how important your knees are for ease of movement. Observe the bones and many muscles and tendons in and around your knees. Breathe into your knees and notice if they become even more relaxed.

Raise your attention to your thighs. Notice if there is tightness in the large muscles of your thighs, the hamstring muscles and quadriceps. Observe these large muscles, the tendons, and the femur, the largest and strongest bone of your body. Breathe into your thighs and notice if they become even more relaxed.

Raise your attention to your hips, buttocks, and pelvic areas. Notice with complete nonjudgment if there is any tension or discomfort anywhere in these areas. Be aware of the large hip bones, the base of your spine, the organs within your abdomen, your genitals, the large muscles of your buttocks, the veins, tendons, and cellular activity. Appreciate how all these areas have served you throughout your life. Breathe into your hip areas and notice if they become even more relaxed.

Become aware of your lower back and stomach. Notice if there is any discomfort or tension in these areas, without judgment, just loving regard. Observe the many organs, muscles, intestines, and your spine in this area. Appreciate the intricacies of the functions of all these organs, muscles, and vertebrae and how they have served you. Breathe into your stomach and lower back and notice if they become even more relaxed and at ease.

Raise your awareness to your chest and upper back. Notice if there is any discomfort in these areas. Be aware of the beating of your heart and how it fuels your entire system with life-giving blood, how it acts as a metaphor for your love. Observe the organs in these areas, the muscles in your chest and upper back, your spine, rib cage, lungs, and all the intricate supporting systems.

Breathe into your chest and upper back and notice if they become even more relaxed.

Be aware of your hands and fingers. Is there any tension in your hands? Look at each finger individually. Observe both sides of your hands, front and back, outside and in, the skin, the muscles, veins, tiny tendons. Appreciate how they have helped you in receiving and giving throughout your life. Be aware of any tension or discomfort in your hands, fingers, and wrists. Observe the many small bones and tiny muscles, tendons, and veins. Breathe into your hands, fingers, and wrists and notice if they become even more relaxed.

Be aware of your wrists without judgment, only loving regard. Observe the entire circumference of your wrists, the skin, muscles, veins, arteries, tiny tendons. Are these precious joints flexible to help in giving and receiving? Be aware of any tension or discomfort in your wrists. Observe the many small bones and tiny muscles, tendons, and veins. Breathe into your wrists and notice if they become even more relaxed.

Be aware of your forearms and elbows. Notice any tension or discomfort, and if it exists, embrace it with love. Be aware of the muscles, skin, veins, bones, and tendons in this region. Give thanks for the flexibility of your elbows that assists you in moving your arms. Breathe into your forearms and elbows and notice if they become even more relaxed.

Be aware of your upper arms, the strong muscles, biceps and lats (latissimus dorsi), and how these parts of your arms have allowed you to lift, move, push, and carry. Be aware of any tension or discomfort in your upper arms. Observe the skin, tendons, veins, and tissue in your upper arms. Breathe into them and notice if they become even more relaxed.

Become aware of your shoulders. Notice any tension or discomfort in this strong area of your body. Notice if there is any burden you have been carrying on your shoulders. Observe the bones, muscles, veins, tendons, and skin in and around your shoulders. Breathe into your shoulders and notice if they melt into deeper relaxation.

Raise your attention to your neck. Notice any tension or discomfort there without judging it but accepting and embracing it with love. Observe all the tiny muscles in your neck and how they move with such synchronized fluidity. Appreciate how your neck has served you in your ability to turn and observe your surroundings, to look over your shoulder and see the past or any danger that may be following you. Observe the skin, tiny bones, and vertebrae, the veins and large arteries, the inside of your throat, the hair on the back of your neck.

Raise your attention to your head and face. Notice if there is any tension in any area of the command center of your body. Be aware of all the special talents possessed in this miracle of anatomy: your ability to see wondrous sights with your eyes, hear the whispering of your beloved with your ears, smell fragrant scents, speak your needs and your wisdom, taste and eat with your mouth. Observe all the intricate functions within your head and face. Scan your chin, the muscles in your face, the inside of your mouth, your tongue, teeth, and gums, your cheeks, nose inside and out, the skin on your face, your ears inside and out, the many components of your hearing apparatus, the tiny muscles in and around your eyes and in your forehead, your scalp and hair. Observe your brain and its connection and moderation of your entire nervous system. Observe all the major areas of the brain—brain stem, cerebellum, cerebrum. Observe the folds of gray matter. Observe the vibrancy of this electrical masterpiece. Breathe deeply into your head and face and notice if it becomes even more relaxed.

Now be aware of your entire body and notice how it all functions together as a whole. Observe your energy body; perhaps you can see it as light and color. See your chakras and intersections of energy lines moving up your spine and to the top of your head. Notice the vibrancy of your energy body, your aura, which radiates many feet beyond your physical body. Breathe into your body and energy body and notice if it becomes even more relaxed and vibrant.

Take as much time as you like in appreciating the magnificence of your body. When it is right for you, take a few deep breaths and return your attention to your surroundings, and when you are ready, open your eyes.

SCRIPTURE MEDITATION

Choose a specific passage in a sacred text or prayer of your choosing. Read the passage several times, ten or more. Reflect on the meaning of the words as you read. After the first several readings, allow the words to sink in at a deeper level than through analysis. Allow them to penetrate your intuitive mind, perhaps even becoming one with the deeper higher meaning of the phrasing. It is often recommended to memorize the passage as you recite it both audibly and inaudibly.

Each time you read the passage, emphasize different words and/or phrases in the passage. You many choose a much longer passage, but here is a short example:

Be still and know that I am *God*.

Be still and know that *I* am God.

Be still and *know* that I am God.

Be *still* and know that I am God.

Be still and know that I am God.

Be still and know that *I am God*.

You can also emphasize and reflect on specific sections of the message:

Be still and know that I am . . .

Be still and know . . .

Be still . . .

Be . . .

Once you have meditated on the words of the passage, close your eyes and allow impressions, images, and feelings to emerge relative to the sacred passage. Remain in this receptive state for as long as it brings you joy to do so. . . . When you are ready, bring your awareness back to the present movement, and when it is right for you, open your eyes. Now reflect on ways you can apply the understanding you have received to your daily life.

WALKING MEDITATION

You can practice walking meditation virtually anytime you are walking. You don't have to set a specific time for it, and it is also quite enjoyable and useful to carve out specific walking meditation time. You can do this indoors or out, but outdoors in nature is especially enjoyable. The labyrinth is a specific type of walking meditation where the walking meditator winds through a circular mazelike path to the center and back again. You can find labyrinths at various locations at www.labyrinthlocator.com. You can set a specific intention for your walking meditation or simply allow the revealing of whatever insight is most appropriate for you at the time of your meditation. Following is a guided walking meditation that can be done indoors, outdoors, in a labyrinth, or simply walking down the street:

Remember the message in this quote by Thich Nhat Hanh

as you begin: "The mind can go in a thousand directions, but on this beautiful path, I walk in peace. With each step, the wind blows. With each step, a flower blooms."

Begin by standing at the beginning of your walking path. Plant your feet firmly on the ground and let your hands rest comfortably at your sides. Become aware of your physical sensations. What do you notice about your body in standing position? Without judgment, just observe. What do you observe about your feeling nature and thought process at this moment in time? Become aware of your surroundings. What do you notice about this place and the sights in and around it?

Begin walking slowly and deliberately with ease and grace, not in a manufactured way, but in a way that feels natural to your inner presence. You can walk in a sacred way as though you were walking on holy ground or to a sacred site. This is not a metaphor. Any time we are walking on Mother Earth, we are on sacred ground. Walk as though you are kissing the Earth with your feet. With each step, feel the sensations of lifting your foot off the Earth. Feel the movements of all the muscles in your body involved in the act of walking. Continue also to be aware of your feelings and thoughts, observing, accepting, and honoring everything you notice.

Be aware of your environment as you move along your path. Notice the intricacies and details of everything you see. You may notice your mind begin to wander, just as it does in seated meditation. Once you notice, observe the thoughts with the same wonder that you observe the beauty and intricacies of your surroundings. Honor your thoughts. Invite them to join you on your walk and observe the beauty of the experience. Whether you are walking back and forth in a shorter area or to one destination and back again, feel your oneness with all life as you observe and honor everything you see and experience.

ZEN TENNIS EXERCISE[2]

You can adapt this exercise to any sport or activity. Just focus on the most central aspect of the task and allow the awareness to gradually move outward until it envelopes the total experience of what you are doing. Most people find this process easy and get into the zone quite effortlessly.

When I had success in tennis lessons with this technique, students would begin to apply all the techniques I had been teaching them without thinking about it. Once I sensed a student was in the zone, I wouldn't say anything. No instruction is needed at that point. There is a time for structured learning and a time for surrendering, so the structured learning can manifest in a non-structured experience in the ever-present now. Some people don't achieve a complete meditative state, but the mere act of watching the ball and being more aware of the tennis experience increases their ability in the moment.

I no longer teach tennis, but I do still play competitively in United States Tennis Association league play. To this day, when I enter the zone, I always play better. Earlier in my career, I would be entering the zone to a large degree in order to win the match, which is not as effective for the meditative state as having no agenda at all other than the joy of being present in the experience. Now I play against my own attachment to winning. When I am fully in the zone, I am completely nonattached. When I am nonattached, I easily and effortlessly enter the meditative zone and ultimately play better and with a greater degree of joy, regardless of the outcome.

Begin by being aware of your body as you are playing. Notice your breathing and the movements of your body. Watch the ball closely as it leaves your opponent's racket. Watch it intently as it comes over the net. Listen closely to the sound of the ball hitting your opponent's racket as well as your own. Watch the rotation of the ball as it comes up and bounces all the way to your strings. (This will improve your performance if you only go this far. Most people don't watch the ball hit their strings.) Watch the ball leave your racket, then focus your attention on your opponent's racket to anticipate the ball coming off its strings once again.

Continue to do this until it becomes natural. Now expand your awareness to include watching not only the ball with complete attention but also the area around the ball. See the lines or cracks on the court as the ball comes up to your strings. See the details of the net as the ball crosses it, but don't decrease your focus on the ball.

When serving, bounce the ball on the ground as you prepare, and watch the ball closely as it hits the ground and comes up to your hand. Observe the writing on the ball, the fuzz, the rotation. As you toss the ball into the air, be aware of the sky without decreasing your focus on the ball. When receiving, closely watch your opponent tossing the ball into the air and the ball coming off the strings of their racket, over the net, and to your racket strings.

Gradually, continue to expand your awareness of your environment to include the clothing of your opponent, the fence around the court, the sights and sounds around the court, birds flying, dogs barking, children playing. Notice the scents in the air, the aroma of flowers or other plant life. Allow yourself to be completely one with the total experience in the moment. Easily and effortlessly slip into the zone of pure joy.

CANDLE MEDITATION

There's not too much to describe for this one. In addition to candles, you can gaze at an object. When out in nature, choose a spot off in the distance, such as a tree or an area on a mountain, and gaze at it. The candle flame is especially conducive to the meditative state because of its hypnotic nature.

Ideally, this meditation can be done at night or in as dark a room as possible, so the light from the candle is more pronounced. Find a comfortable spot and place and light a candle that is on a surface at eye level, or on the floor several feet from you, so you don't have to tilt your head too far forward.

Gaze at the candle, allowing it to capture your full attention and imagination. Notice how easily your gaze brings you into the light. You may even feel like you are becoming one with the flame. As with other meditation forms, you will most likely have thoughts come into play. Invite them into the candle meditation. Invite the thoughts into the light, into your now sacred relationship with the candle flame. Continue gazing into the candle for as long as it brings you joy and peace. . . .

Complete the exercise with reflection on your light and how you want to share it with the world. Below is a poem I wrote about thirty-three years ago that relates to the candle meditation and to all the meditation practices in this book:

The Fires of My Mind

The fires of my mind are not meant to be wisped about
by the winds of the will of others.
Nor are they to be consumed by the flames of social thinking.
Nor are they to be doused by the waters of emotional turbulence.
They remain but a single flame held steady in the light of my soul.
Flickering only in harmony with divine purpose.
Lighting the way.[3]

COLOR CYCLE

This exercise can be used as a meditation by itself or as an entrance into any of the meditations discussed. The act of snapping your fingers and switching from one color to the next creates a body-mind connection. Feel free to experiment with snapping your fingers or not to see which works best for you. Once you reach the state of "white," you can go into another meditative practice or do healing work, all within the center of your mind.

Take a deep breath and hold it to a slow count of four or longer. . . . Release your breath, snap your fingers, and be in red. Completely surround yourself in the vibrant color of red. If you're not very visual, just imagine what it would feel like to be surrounded by the bright color of red. You can also imagine a bright red apple and then see and feel that color all around you. Feel yourself becoming one with the vibration of red.

Take another deep breath and hold it to the same slow count of four. . . . Release your breath, snap your fingers, and be in orange. See and feel yourself surrounded by the warm, comforting color of orange. Feel yourself becoming one with the vibration of orange.

Take another deep breath and hold it. . . . Release your breath, snap your fingers, and be in yellow. See and feel yourself completely surrounded in the warm, calming color of yellow. Feel mellow yellow all around you. Feel yourself becoming one with the vibration of yellow.

Take another deep breath, hold it, tighten your jaw muscles, raise your eyes to the top of your head. . . . Release your breath, relax your facial muscles, snap your fingers, and be in the healing color of green. Feel a tingling sensation at the top of your head, then moving down through your entire body, bringing a wave of relaxation and healing. You have now reached a point of complete physical relaxation as you become one with the healing vibration of green.

Take another deep breath and hold it. . . . Release your breath, snap your fingers, and be in the tranquil color of blue. Feel your emotional nature becoming calmer and calmer until you reach a point of complete emotional tranquility, like a completely motionless blue woodland pool, with a surface as smooth as glass. You have now reached a point of complete emotional peace as you become one with the vibration of blue.

Take another deep breath and hold it. . . . Release your breath, snap your fingers, and be in the peaceful color of indigo (the color of the sky at dawn). Feel all your mental processes slowing down. Slower and slower and slower, until you reach a point of complete mental stillness, like an indigo flame held steady in the light of your soul as you become one with the vibration of indigo.

Take another deep breath and hold it. . . . Release your breath, snap your fingers, and be in the magical color of violet. Feel yourself aligned with your own inner magnificence as you become one with the vibration of violet.

Take another deep breath and hold it. . . . Release your breath, snap your fingers, and be in white, at the very center of your mind, the center of infinite mind. This is the place where all things are possible. Continue to simply be in white and this state of oneness for as long as you like or move into another meditative form. . . . When you are ready, bring your awareness back, feeling better than ever before.

MOUNTAINTOP MEDITATION[4]

Breathe deeply, filling your lungs with air all the way down to your abdomen. Exhale completely. With each breath, feel yourself becoming more relaxed, at peace, and aligned with your highest potential—dwelling in love. Imagine that you are standing on a mountaintop at dawn. The sun has not yet appeared in the East, but its soft glow is peeking above the horizon. The air is cool and crisp, yet completely comfortable, and there is magic in the air. You are in harmony with your surroundings. You can hear the animal life in the bushes and trees around you. You feel connected with everything in your environment: the four-legged, the crawlers, flyers in the sky, swimmers in the river below, the plant people, the stone people, the mountain itself, Mother Earth, and Father Sky.

The first ray of the sun appears on the horizon and streams toward you, landing right in your heart. Something magical is happening. Your body becomes lighter and lighter, and you begin to lift off of the mountaintop. You realize that you are no longer in physical form. Your consciousness is contained within a bubble of thin moisture. You lift off the Earth into the night sky. As you rise higher and higher, your awareness contained in the bubble becomes lighter and lighter and the walls of the bubble get thinner and thinner. Your awareness includes more and more space as the bubble expands faster than it is rising. It envelops the mountaintop, then the entire mountain, the valleys below, other mountain ranges, land masses, and bodies of water. The entire Earth is now within the bubble of your consciousness, getting smaller and smaller as you expand. Continuing to expand, your bubble envelops nearby planets, the sun from which that first magical ray streamed forth, the entire solar system, the Milky Way, other galaxies, the universe, other universes. The bubble of your awareness is so stretched that it becomes unstable, in a good way. Finally, the walls of the bubble become so thin, they can no longer contain your consciousness and ever so gently dissolve with a silent *pop*, and your awareness is released to stretch through the infinite universe. Allow your awareness to be . . . limitless . . . unbounded by mental constraints . . . free . . . just being . . . one with all. . . .

Take as much time as you like in this state of pure bliss, and whenever you are ready, slowly and gently bring your awareness back to your environment. Become aware of your body, grounding the infinite peace, love, and light that you have experienced. Feel it coursing through your veins, beating in your heart, sinking deep into your cells, grounding into Mother Earth through your feet. When it's right for you, bring your awareness all the way back, take a deep breath, and open your eyes.

POWER ANIMAL

Breathe deeply, filling your lungs with air all the way down to your abdomen. Exhale completely. With each breath, feel yourself becoming more relaxed, at peace, aligned with your highest potential, in love and light. Imagine that you are in a nature place, a place that is relaxing and peaceful. It could be a mountaintop, a meadow filled with wildflowers, near a waterfall, the beach. Use all your senses to appreciate your beautiful surroundings. Touch the plant life. Smell the sweet aromas in the air. Observe the various colors all around you. Take your time and enjoy every second of your experience. . . .

Now look around for a place that is your personal power spot—a place where the energy has been prepared perfectly just for you. The exact qualities that you need for your highest healing, revitalization, and perfect balance are supplied in the energy of this spot. When you find it, sit down in your power spot and take some time to allow that perfect energy to wash through you—balancing your being into perfect health and harmony. . . .

As you are meditating in your power spot, you begin to feel a presence. You instantly know it is the presence of your power animal. Open your inner eyes and look into the eyes of your power animal, which is now standing right in front of you. It could be any kind of animal, one that represents power to you. Look deeply into your power animal's eyes—into the soul of this great being. Acclimate your breath to the same rhythm of your power animal until you are breathing with it in perfect harmony. Feel your heart beating in rhythm with the heart of your power animal. Now feel your consciousness moving into the body of your power animal. Feel the strength and grace in your powerful body looking at yourself through the eyes of your power animal. What do you see?

Now your animal takes off on a symbolic journey of your life through your nature place. Be aware of your surroundings. Look for images that may have symbolic meaning as your power animal chooses the path that will bring you the most beneficial teaching. How does it feel to travel in the body of your power animal? How do you face challenges as your power animal? Do you worry about outcomes or simply respond instinctively? How do you decide what path to take? Does it require deliberation, or do you *know* intuitively? Take as much time as you need to complete your journey. . . .

When you have completed your journey, go back to where your personality still sits. Look into your eyes again through the eyes of your power animal. Is there anything you want to communicate to yourself through the thoughts of your power animal? Allow your consciousness to move back into your own body so that you are again looking through your own eyes at your power animal. Thank your power animal for teaching you about power. Say goodbye to your power animal and take a final look around at your nature place. Realize that you can come back to this place anytime you like. You can call on the strength and wisdom of your power animal at any point in time.

Decide what you would like to take with you from this place back into your daily life. Take a few moments to decide how you can use this experience in your life and how you can contribute to the growth of others through your thoughts, feelings, actions, and words. . . .

Take as much time as you like in this exploration, and whenever you are ready, slowly and gently bring your awareness back to your environment. Become aware of your body, grounding the infinite peace, love, and power that you have experienced. Feel it coursing through your veins, beating in your heart, sinking deep into your cells, grounding into Mother Earth through your feet. When it's right for you, bring your awareness all the way back, take a deep breath, and open your eyes.

SUN MEDITATION[5]

Breathe deeply, filling your lungs with air all the way down to your abdomen. Exhale completely. With each breath, feel yourself becoming more relaxed, at peace, aligned with your highest potential, in love and light. Imagine you are standing on the highest mountaintop and gazing out at the world in all directions. To the east is the rising sun. You feel its loving warmth on your skin. Drink in the sunshine with your pores and pay homage to the sun spirit with your mind and soul. Be aware of a single golden ray streaming forth from the sun and enveloping you. Feel the sunlight transforming your body as it bathes you outside and within. Your body becomes lighter as though it is becoming the light of the ray itself. Your molecular structure changes as you become sunlight. Your awareness is now traveling through the sunbeam toward the sun. As you approach the heavenly orb, the light becomes more intense and the life-giving energy purer. You are not afraid because you are of the same nature as the sun. As you enter the sun's atmosphere, your consciousness explodes and becomes one with the sun. What does it feel like to be the sun, radiating love and life in all directions? Feel the power as your awareness envelops all that the light from the sun reaches. Feel the enormity of your consciousness.

Now be aware of your personality back on Earth. As the sun, a symbol of your soul, observe your personality in its daily activities. What do you see from this high perspective? What message would you like to communicate to your earthly self? Communicate it through your light. How do you feel as the sun when your personality has blocked your light with clouds of doubt or fear? What is your message to yourself in these times? Communicate that message with your light. What other messages, encouragement, or qualities do you want to send to your personal self on Earth?

Allow your awareness to focus on your personality and be aware of that one golden stream of light that connects you to your body. Allow your awareness to travel through the beam, bringing the nurturing love of the sun, of your soul, through the stream to your personality. Say your name over and over as you approach your body. Bring the love and perspective into your body and feel it in your heart. Breathe deeply as you fully accept the love and support of your soul consciousness. . . .

Take as much time as you like in this state of pure bliss, and whenever you are ready, slowly and gently bring your awareness back to your environment. Become aware of your body, grounding the infinite peace, love, and light that you have experienced. Feel it coursing through your veins, beating in your heart, sinking deep into your cells, grounding into Mother Earth through your feet. When it's right for you, bring your awareness all the way back, take a deep breath, and open your eyes.

THE TEMPLE

Breathe deeply, filling your lungs with air all the way down to your abdomen. Exhale completely. With each breath feel yourself becoming more relaxed, at peace, aligned with your highest potential, in love and light. Imagine that you are walking through the Himalayas in Tibet. Look around you at all the beautiful scenery. Use all your senses to explore your environment. Smell the fresh pine trees and other plant life. Observe the majesty of the snow-capped mountains. Feel the crisp air on your skin. Sense the magical quality of the energy that fills you and exists all around you. As you walk along a path through the valley, you see ahead of you a forest snuggled against the base of the largest mountain. There is something alluring about the forest, something profound and mystical. As you move a little closer, you notice there is a faint light coming from deep within the forest. The closer you get, the brighter the light becomes and you feel something in you beginning to change. You are going deeper into a state of heightened awareness. As you approach the forest, you can see the light streaming through the trees, glistening off the leaves and pine needles. There is a deer path leading into the forest. Clearly, humans have traveled this path before, but not for many years. You begin down the path and again feel your awareness going deeper and becoming lighter and freer. The farther you travel into the forest, the brighter the streams of light become, making their way through the dense trees.

Finally, you begin to approach a clearing and can see glimpses of the source of the light—an ancient temple. Observe the temple closely as you step into the clearing. Is your temple elaborate and ornate, or is it simple and humble? Begin to walk into the light streaming from the temple as you approach its door. Place your hand on the handle and sense what might be inside. Open the door and walk inside. The interior of the temple is lit with thousands of candle flames, but this is not the source of the light you have followed from this place. At the center of the temple is a beam of light reaching up through the ceiling into the heavens and down through the floor deep into Mother Earth. Approach the beam of light and again feel yourself moving deeper into that heightened state. You can sense that the energy in this beam of light contains the qualities that you most need to balance your being into perfect harmony and optimal health. Step into the beam of light and kneel or sit in meditation as you receive those qualities. Allow yourself to let go completely and absorb this perfect energy. Simply receive the support and love that you deserve. . . .

Take as much time as you need in this state of receptive freedom and then reflect on how you can use the energy and qualities you received in your daily life. How can you increase the quality of your life and those you influence through your thoughts, feelings, words, and actions? When you have completed this process, stand and decide what you would like to take back from your temple. Recognize that you can return to this place any time you wish simply by willing yourself here.

Whenever you are ready, slowly and gently bring your awareness back to your environment. Become aware of your body, grounding the infinite peace, love, and light that you have experienced. Feel it coursing through your veins, beating in your heart, sinking deep into your cells, grounding into Mother Earth through your feet. When it's right for you, bring your awareness all the way back, take a deep breath, and open your eyes.

WISE BEING

Breathe deeply, filling your lungs with air all the way down to your abdomen. Exhale completely. With each breath, feel yourself becoming more relaxed, at peace, aligned with your highest potential, in love and light. Imagine that you are in a beautiful place in nature. Look around you and explore your surrounding with all your senses. Touch the plant life. Smell the sweet aromas in the air. Observe the various colors all around you. Take your time and enjoy every second of your experience. . . . Now look far off into the distance. You see a figure that you can barely make out coming toward you and you know instantly that this is the form of your wise being—a being that possesses perfect strength, love, compassion, and wisdom. It could be a spiritual figure, a Buddha or Christ, a great teacher, someone you know, a mythical figure, or an abstract image representing wisdom. Walk toward the image as it moves toward you. As you get closer, you begin to see the image more clearly. Finally, the image is close enough that you can make out the features. When the image is close enough, look directly into the eyes of your wise being. Sense the compassion, power, and wisdom of this holy being. Ask your wise being any question you would like to. If the answers are not completely clear, ask for clarification. Dialogue with your wise being on any issue that is relevant in your life at this time. . . . Ask your wise being what is necessary for your next step in growth. . . . Now feel your consciousness moving into your wise being until you are looking at yourself through the compassionate eyes of your wise being. How do you view yourself from this position of compassion and clarity? How does it feel to experience the qualities of wisdom and compassion? Take some time to appreciate this sensation. Is there anything you would like to say to yourself with the voice of your wise being? Now move your consciousness back into your body, taking with you the peace and wisdom from your wise being. When you are back in your body, recognize that all the qualities of your wise being are also part of you. The fact that you can create this being in your imagination illustrates that the wise being is in you. Thank your wise being for guiding you. Look around at your nature place and know that you can return here anytime you wish simply by visualizing it. Take a few moments to decide how you can use this experience in your life and how you can contribute to the growth of others through your thoughts, feelings, actions, and words. When you are through, take a deep breath and open your eyes, feeling better than ever.

THE PATH OF LIGHT

Breathe deeply, filling your lungs with air all the way down to your abdomen. Exhale completely. With each breath, feel yourself becoming more relaxed, at peace, aligned with your highest potential, in love and light. Imagine before you a golden path of light. At the end of the path, off in the distance, is a symbol of your highest understanding of the Divine, Spirit, the Mystery. It could be a spiritual or religious being, an abstract image, a golden sphere of pure light. Slowly walk down the golden path toward this highest symbol of the Divine. The farther down the path you walk, the more you begin to feel the presence and energy of this Divine emanation. As you come closer, you feel Its energy enveloping and infusing your entire being. Your own energy begins to vibrate at the frequency of this Powerful Presence. As you approach this Divine Presence, it becomes difficult to distinguish yourself from the pervasive presence of this Being. You are now as close as you can be, right next to the Presence. You pause, basking in the light, love, and grace of this Holy Presence. Now step into the sphere of this Being, and become one with It. You now are the Presence, radiating love, light, and power in all directions. Remain in the consciousness of pure light, love, and power—radiating, sustaining all life, being pure bliss. All life is contained within the sphere of your infinite magnificence. . . .

Take as much time as you like in this state of pure bliss, and whenever you are ready, slowly and gently bring your awareness back to your environment. Become aware of your body, grounding the infinite peace, love, and light that you have experienced. Feel it coursing through your veins, beating in your heart, sinking deep into your cells, grounding deep into Mother Earth. When it's right for you, bring your awareness all the way back, take a deep breath, and open your eyes.

SHORT-FORM DAILY MEDITATION

For those who don't feel they have time to meditate for fifteen, twenty minutes or more, this meditation can be done in as little as three minutes. It can also be used by those who normally meditate longer but sometimes have less time. If you spend only three minutes (or one minute, for that matter) in meditation each morning, it is infinitely better than not meditating at all.

Once again, make sure that you are ready to meditate:

- Prepare your space so it is calm and tranquil.

- Turn off your phone.

- Tell others in your environment that you are having quiet time and to please not disturb.

- Make sure the temperature is comfortable.

- Visit the bathroom if applicable before beginning so your physical comfort will be maintained.

- Make sure your journal is close by if you choose to use one to write down pressing thoughts that may come up during meditation, so you can write them down and return to meditation with a freer mind.

- Set a timer if you have a prescribed amount of time that you want to meditate, so you don't have to be checking or thinking about the time.

Begin by taking a deep breath and letting out a nice big heartful sigh. Continue to breathe deeply.... After a few deep breaths, visualize yourself going through your daily activities, accomplishing whatever you want to accomplish in this day. See yourself going about your tasks with focus, freedom, ease, and joy. What other qualities do you want present during your activities today? Feel them in your heart and in the hearts of others you will interact with. Visualize yourself laying down to sleep at the end of the day with a feeling of accomplishment, gladness, and peace....

Now take a few moments of silence, observe your thoughts, focus on your breathing, repeat an inner mantra, chant out loud, or use any other techniques you've practiced or learned through this reading to move into mindfulness and/or silent mind. As you notice thoughts, sensations, or feelings coming into play, simply observe them. Invite them into the peace and bliss and return to your practice of watching your breath, inner mantra, chanting, or any other practice that takes you deep....

Take as much time as you like in this state of pure bliss, and whenever you are ready, slowly and gently bring your awareness back to your environment. Become aware of your body, grounding the infinite peace, love, and light that you have experienced. Feel it coursing through your veins, beating in your heart, sinking deep into your cells, grounding deep into Mother Earth. When it's right for you, bring your awareness all the way back, take a deep breath, and open your eyes.

LONGER-FORM DAILY MEDITATION

Once again, make sure that you are ready to meditate:

- Prepare your space so it is calm and tranquil.

- Turn off your phone.

- Tell others in your environment that you are having quiet time and to please not disturb.

- Make sure the temperature is comfortable.

- Visit the bathroom if applicable before beginning so your physical comfort will be maintained.

- Make sure your journal is close by if you choose to use one to write down pressing thoughts that may come up during meditation, so you can write them down and then return to meditation with a freer mind.

- Set a timer if you have a prescribed amount of time that you want to meditate, so you don't have to be checking or thinking about the time.

The following is an example of one form of daily meditation you can use, but feel free to create your own, mixing and matching from the practices offered in this book and/or creating your own to add to your meditation journey.

You can begin with the Color Cycle described earlier, moving from each color of the rainbow to the next and then into white, or one of the many guided imagery examples, or start with deep breathing, or the body scan, or dive right into mindfulness or the still-mind techniques of watching the breath, inner mantra, and chanting. Or begin with the daily intention setting just like in the Short-Form Daily Meditation, and/or add the following not previously described practice that is a personal favorite as well:

Begin by taking a deep breath and let out a big heartful sigh. Continue to breathe deeply. With each breath, feel yourself becoming more relaxed, centered, aligned, at peace, in love. . . . Visualize yourself going through your daily activities accomplishing whatever you want to accomplish in this day. See yourself doing so with focus, freedom, ease, and joy. What other qualities do you want present during your activities today? Feel them in your heart and in the hearts of others you will interact with. Visualize yourself lying down to sleep at the end of the day with a feeling of accomplishment, gladness, and peace. . . .

Now feel your crown chakra (at the top of your head) opening and receiving pure light and love from Spirit. This light illuminates your entire being. Now feel your heart chakra opening wide, allowing the love and light to flow and radiate from it. Feel it pouring out into your environment. If indoors, it fills the room, then the entire building. The love and light expands outward, spanning the entire city, bringing with it a healing vibration to everything and everyone it touches. It continues to expand, stretching across the state or province, the country, the continent, oceans, land masses, until it spans the entire planet, creating a blanket of love and light illuminating the entire world.

Now feel your personal identity dissolving into the light and love that has been flowing through you. Become the light and love. Observe your thoughts, focus on your breathing, repeat an inner mantra, chant out loud, or use any other techniques you've practiced or learned to move into mindfulness and/or silent mind. As you notice thoughts, sensations, or feelings coming into play, simply observe them, invite them into the peace and bliss, and return to your practice of watching your breath, inner mantra, chanting, or any other practice that takes you deep. Take as much time in this surrendering meditation as feels right to you. . . .

Continue to recognize yourself as an energy of love, light, and healing. Focus on family members, friends, and/or people who have requested prayer or healing energy, and direct love and light to them. Or simply say a prayer for them. See them in their perfected state, whole, healthy, abundant, and peaceful.

Close with a prayer of your choice. The following is an ancient prayer called "The Great Invocation." I have modified the language to make it more universal, gender neutral, and positive:

The Great Invocation (revised)

From the point of Light within the Mind of God
Let light stream forth into the minds of all.
Let Light descend on Earth.
From the point of Love within the heart of God
Let love stream forth into the hearts of all
May the coming One appear.
From the center where the Will of God is known
Let purpose guide the little wills of all—
The purpose which the Masters know and serve.
From the center which we call the human race
Let the Plan of Love and Light work out
And may it heal the realms where darkness dwells.
Let Light and Love and Power restore the Plan on Earth.

Continue to remain in a state of radiant love and light for as long as you wish. Take as much time as you like in this state of bliss, and whenever you are ready, slowly and gently bring your awareness back to your environment. Become aware of your body, grounding the infinite peace, love, and light that you have experienced. Feel it coursing through your veins, beating in your heart, sinking deep into your cells, grounding deep into Mother Earth. When it's right for you, bring your awareness all the way back, take a deep breath, and open your eyes.

{ 5 }

SUPPORTING SPIRITUAL PRACTICES

Virtually everyone who embarks on a meditation path and makes it a priority in their life discovers techniques to augment their meditation practice and keep the inner peace present as an ongoing experience. This chapter presents several classical practices, as well as modern techniques and others that I have developed or modified for my own use and to share with others.

AFFIRMATION

You can create affirmations for anything you want to change about yourself or your life. Your affirmations are seeds that will grow into new behaviors and patterns. Moisten the soil with the water of your positive feelings that corresponds to the seeds of your affirmations. It may take time for the confidence to come that will inspire new ways of being, just as it takes time for a plant to take root and grow. Trust and be patient.

Stop reading for a moment and consider what quality you need most in your life. Create a short phrase that affirms you already possess it. Make it an "I" statement: "I am powerful." "I am loving." "I am wildly abundant." The affirmation is the truth because you do possess the quality in your soul or potential. The affirmation will be like a magnet drawing power into your subconscious mind and, ultimately, your reality. Repeat the affirmation over and over. If it will bring you joy to do so, commit to saying the affirmation a minimum of fifty times a day. Or simply say it a few times as part of your daily meditation practice. Write notes or signs to yourself containing your affirmation and place them where you will see them often.

Every positive thought creates strength, healing, and light for the thinker and fosters a nurturing effect on all life. Accept yourself the way you are and recognize that you can take a major step forward in this moment. You can choose a much more powerful way to use your mind.

You can also use your mind to affirm empowerment for others. When someone is talking to you about their problems, you can empower them (even if they are in denial or want to remain stuck in the problem) by refusing to buy into the problem. You can do this with compassion and, at the same time, affirm in your mind their ability to solve their problems. Sometimes it is more effective to do this without communicating it, because the disclosure may meet with resistance, and the affirmation can have a positive effect even without their conscious knowledge.

PRAYER

It has been said that prayer is the act of talking to God, and meditation is the act of listening. It's always nice to have a two-way conversation. My wife prays and meditates each morning. Prayer can be part of a meditation practice and, of course, can be an all-day practice. Prayer can be offered to the One Presence many call God or to various saints, masters, deities from various religions, or avatars (divine incarnations), such as Jesus Christ in Christianity and Krishna in Hinduism and Vedic traditions.

Like meditation, prayer can be done at any time and throughout one's day. As a child I remember having an ongoing conversation with God as I understood God to be at that level of mental development. That reminds me of a question my first spiritual teacher in adulthood asked once: "Is your concept of God now the same as it was at five years old? Did God change or did your understanding evolve?" Our concept of God and everything else naturally evolves as we evolve. In the Bible it says, "You are created in God's image." What is equally true is that we create our god in our own image. If we believe in a punishing, vengeful world, we will most likely believe in a punishing, vengeful god. If we believe that love is the nature of our world, we will most likely create a loving god.

I suppose I still have conversations with God, although my understanding has evolved substantially. I also often ask my angels for assistance. I call them "angels" because I like the image. My clearer understanding, however, is that there are helping energies and beings on the inner planes around us at all times. Their primary purpose is to assist humans in the evolution of consciousness and the expression of love. When I ask for guidance or assistance, they usually ask me more questions, like "What do you really want?" Their questions help me become clearer and therefore more effective in attracting what I want.

AFFIRMATIVE PRAYER

Affirmative prayer is different than petitioning prayer. Rather than praying to a higher power outside of oneself for what we want to experience in life, affirmative prayer assumes that since we are one with God or a Higher Power, we don't need to petition benevolence or grace from a being outside ourselves, but simply to state that whatever we want is our divine right as expressions of The One. Our good is already within us. Of course, you can use petitioning prayer and affirmative prayer concurrently or periodically depending on your perspective at the time.

The Science of Mind, based on the book by Ernest Holmes, offers a five-step method to affirmative prayer called "spiritual mind treatment." Following are simple examples of the five steps to help guide you. In practice, the steps can be modified and elaborated upon.

1. **Recognition:** I recognize there is one Infinite Presence of Light, Love, and Peace.

2. **Unification:** I am one with this Infinite Presence. I am a perfect expression of this Light, Love, Peace, and Abundance.

3. **Realization:** I recognize that as an expression of the Divine, I already possess everything that I want and need (state specifically what you want—perfect health, prosperity, healthy relationships, right livelihood, etc.).

4. **Thanksgiving:** I give thanks for all the blessings in life and for the manifestation of this prayer that has already been accomplished in mind, feeling, and energy.

5. **Release:** I release this prayer into the field of potential that always says yes. I let it go completely with trust and faith that it is done. And so it is.

VISUALIZATION

Visualization can be a part of a meditation practice and can also be done for the purpose of facilitating a life of greater joy, peace, contentment, and enlightenment. Whatever it is you most want to create in your life, you can visualize. There are many sayings that illustrate the power of visualization. This simple one sums it up nicely: "If you can see it, you can be it." It is true that for anything we do well, we first have an image of ourselves doing it, whether we are conscious of that or not.

It is commonplace in recent times and as a result of research, for top athletes to use visualization techniques to enhance their performance in sports. In his book *For the Love of the Game*, Michael Jordan cites his natural ability to visualize as a contributing factor in his unprecedented success in basketball: "I have used visualization techniques for as long as I can remember. I always visualized my success. It wasn't until later in my career that I realized the technique is something that most people have to learn. I had been practicing the principles naturally my entire life. I visualized how many points I was going to score, how I was going to score them, how I was going to break down my opponent."[1]

His uncanny natural ability is likely a major reason for his tremendous success in becoming perhaps the greatest professional basketball player ever and possibly the greatest professional athlete ever—certainly one of the most celebrated.

Try using visualization to improve anything you wish to learn or achieve. Simply close your eyes and imagine yourself performing the task perfectly and effortlessly. People who are not naturally visual can still be successful using this technique. If you struggle with *seeing* the images internally, perhaps you are more auditory or kinesthetic in the way you process information. In this case, try adding the sounds that would represent the perfect, effortless accomplishment to the internal experience. Try *feeling* what it would be like to accomplish the goal or activity perfectly and effortlessly. During your visualizations, affirm that you are performing the task or the accomplishment in the present moment in your mind. In other words, rather than projecting the image into the future, imagine that you are experiencing it in the now moment.

Over the years, I have used visualization techniques to improve athletic performance, prepare speeches, and create joyful and successful experiences in my daily life. When I prepare for a speech, workshop, or retreat, I close my eyes and visualize how I want the experience to be for myself and for those in attendance. I add feeling to the scenario. What feelings do I want myself and my audiences to experience? I feel those emotions in the moment. I complete by affirming that what I have visualized and felt has already been manifested in mind and heart and that showing up in the world of form is a mere form-ality. Then when I am in the midst of offering my services, I simply let go and let my vision unfold naturally.

I highly recommend practicing this technique for any important event of your life: taking a test, interviewing for a job, proposing to your boyfriend or girlfriend, performing a sport, having a medical procedure. For this last example, imagine the procedure going perfectly. The doctor or health professional's consciousness is in the perfect space to perform masterfully, and his or her hands are guided by Spirit, highest potential, the hands of God, your higher self, or whatever terms you prefer.

MINDFULNESS

Mindfulness is not only a meditation technique, it is, in fact, a way of life. Just as we can aspire to be in a meditative state at any moment in time, we can also be mindful in any and all circumstances. The more mindful we are, the more peace, love, and inner joy we can live in and from.

Take a moment to glance up from the page after reading this sentence and take note of what is around you.... See if you can notice details about your environment that you would miss if you were not looking in a mindful way.... Continue to observe your environment mindfully after each sentence, or every other sentence if you choose, or read to the end of the paragraph and then practice the following suggestions. Even if you are in a familiar place, I'll bet you can notice things you have never noticed before.... Look carefully at the objects or scenery if you are outside and notice what you notice. "Notice" sounds both obvious and subtle. See if you can learn something from the objects you see. Choose one particular object and look as deeply as you can into its nature. What message does it have to offer you from its way of being?

When you return your awareness to reading these words, see if you are in a more expanded state of consciousness. See if you are more receptive to the material that you're reading. So many spiritual teachings focus on being present in the moment. We spend much of our mental energy fretting about the past or worrying about the future. In the words of the title of Ram Dass's famous book, *Be Here Now*, this doesn't mean we can't learn from the past and focus our intention on the future. It means we bring them into the present moment while being present to what's happening around us as opposed to getting lost in the past or future.

BE THE OBJECTIVE OBSERVER

Being the observer is a practical way of applying mindfulness. Once again, the metaphor of what works in meditation works in life. In this practice we simply observe whatever is happening externally and, most important, inwardly. I can observe what is happening in general in my life from a nonattached perspective.

If I am in a situation or interacting with someone who is triggering an uncomfortable feeling for me, such as fear, sadness, pain, anger, or even rage, I can aspire to observe the situation and my feelings as much as possible, even if I am reacting in a way I wish I wasn't. The more proficient we become at being the objective observer, the more we become aligned with our higher potential and the more likely we are to respond from a more peaceful and enlightened presence. And when we are not able to do so, by being the observer, we will learn more from the situation than if we are completely lost in our reactive emotion. And we can be the observer in retrospect as well. Look back over your daily activities, especially those that elicit strong reactions, and review them without judgment.

Try this now, while you are reading. Be aware of what you are thinking as you read the words on the page. What are your thoughts about the material you are reading? Are you taking it in and absorbing it? Are you thinking, "This is the most enlightened material I've ever read"? Are you thinking, "This stuff is pretty strange," or "This author doesn't know what he's talking about!"? Are you thinking, "Maybe I should skip this last chapter and go meditate"? Whatever you are thinking, observe the thoughts.

Be aware of what you are feeling inside as you read the words on the page. Are you feeling curious, board, angry, enthused, excited, intrigued? Whatever the feeling, observe it without judgment, and just watch. Are there sounds around you that you weren't aware of? See if you can observe the sounds while you continue to read.

To take this into a daily practice, for the next seven days and nights, observe your thoughts, feelings, actions, words, and interactions with others. Don't necessarily try to change anything. Just observe. Changes will come naturally and easily.

RADICAL GRATITUDE

After the publication of my first book, I traveled extensively lecturing about what I call "radical gratitude." We're all aware of the benefits of being grateful for what we have. Grateful for our blessings and the many joys in our lives—that's regular gratitude. Radical gratitude is being grateful for the situations and experiences in life that challenge us the most. What I found in espousing this idea eighteen years ago was a lot of "ahas" in the audiences I spoke to. Now what I find is lots of heads nodding up and down.

Radical gratitude is a concept that has become part of the collective consciousness. Our most popular and celebrated spiritual teachers and authors are all saying the same thing in different ways. Byron Katie says to love everything, every experience, every person, no matter what; Eckhart Tolle encourages people to give up resistance to what is; Robert Scheinfeld in *Busting Loose from the Money Game* (a favorite book of mine that isn't about money but consciousness) says, "Appreciate everything"; August Gold and Joel Fotinos in *The Prayer Chest* say, "Invite everything, every experience"; and in *The Magic of the Soul*, I say, "Look for the magic in everything, every situation, especially the most challenging ones."

There is a quote that I love that is attributed to the Buddha that perhaps he never said. I only know this because when I first saw the quote, I googled it to make sure I had the wording correct and was directed to a page with a picture of the Buddha and a caption that read, "I didn't say that!" The page contained a list of all the sayings incorrectly attributed to the Buddha. The quote is as follows: "When you realize how perfect everything is, you will tilt your head back and laugh at the sky." Can you feel the peace and power in that?

In my writing and lectures I share about the experience of writing *The Magic of the Soul*, how it ultimately became a successful publishing project, and how the message evolved. I started out writing a book with an emphasis on how to manifest what you want in life. I felt I was pretty darn good at manifestation. I had a great job as a director for Sage Publications, a world-renowned social science publishing house. I had a wonderful marriage of thirteen years. I was in excellent health and condition, having been a tennis pro in my twenties and a martial artist in my thirties.

A funny thing happened on the way to the magic of the soul. Everything fell apart. I became chronically ill with no diagnosis for three years. My marriage of thirteen years ended, and my great corporate job went away. Everything I had identified with on a personal or ego-level basis had been stripped away in about six months. The chronic illness lasted for three years with no progress. I availed myself of virtually every traditional and alternative healing intervention for three years with no improvement and with no specific diagnosis. In fact, the symptoms were increasing. I was bedridden for weeks at a time and was beginning to think I was approaching the end of this earth-plane existence. All the while I resisted the experience and the symptoms.

Then what happened is I gave up. Not in an apathetic sense, but in a surrendering way. I decided that if I was going to die from this, if I was nearing the end of this life journey, I was going to use the experience of dying to understand at the deepest level who I am as a sacred being. So guess what happened? Yes, I began to heal, slowly at first, but that healing did not occur in a straight line. I would start to feel better and go out and do things that I used to be able to do, like take a walk, and it would put me back in bed again. Again, I would resist the symptoms, maybe even more so, because it felt so good to feel even just a little bit better, and the symptoms would worsen. Then I would remember, "Oh yes, it was that surrendering thing that had me feeling better." So I would surrender again.

It was like my soul was teaching me in the most direct and dynamic way possible about learning to be in a consistent state of surrender. What would your life be like in a consistent state of surrender?

The message of the book took a new turn. Rather than merely pointing out that it is magical to create what we want, the message crafted from my experience of writing the book (or perhaps the book writing me) became to appreciate the magic in what we have. And not just those things in life that bring us happiness, but especially the things that create discomfort or challenge us the most. As conscious beings, when we look back over our lives, we tend to recognize that our most challenging times in life are the times we grow the most. We may even say in retrospect the dark time was a blessing in disguise. But how do we respond to challenges or discomfort in the moment? We resist it, yes? What I am suggesting is to appreciate the blessing in the moment. If we can't see the blessing, we can at least trust that there is one.

As the practice of radical gratitude or looking for the magic in every experience has evolved for me, life has become progressively sweeter. There is rarely any fear, resistance, or attachment to anything. Since I found surrender and a deeper understanding of the truth and love of which my being consists, what more could there be to fear? If I know that no matter what occurs for me (because nothing happens *to* us and everything happens *for* us) is for my highest good, then everything that happens is truly "all good."

To sum it up, here's one of my all-time favorite quotes from Pam Grout in *E³: Nine More Energy Experiments That Prove Manifesting Magic and Miracles Is Your Full-Time Gig*: "Once you can say, 'This is the best thing to happen to me' about everything that happens in your life, you'll be aligned with the FP [field of potential]. . . ."[2] "You align with the FP by loving everyone, by seeing the 'face of God' in everything, by feeling happy, by being joyful and grateful for everything no matter what. Instead of letting the 'apparent reality' dictate your feelings, you line up with the FP, which knows nothing but love, peace, and perfect contentment."[3]

NONATTACHMENT

Another hallmark of Buddhist practice is nonattachment. Interestingly enough, in my experience, the practice of looking for the magic in every situation or for the greater freedom, joy, love, etc. that wants to emerge from every challenging situation naturally leads to nonattachment. If I truly believe that everything is happening for me and nothing happens *to* me or is against me, then there is nothing to fear about the future. This doesn't mean that I don't ever have fear come up in my life, but as a result of these practices, it is maybe 2 percent of the time, whereas before these practices, even after meditating for twenty years, fear was present more consistently, occasionally a somewhat intense fear, and more consistently a subtler sense that something bad may happen, or when things are going well, "When is the other shoe going to drop?"

What I've found is that the only way to true and lasting peace is to be at least relatively nonattached to outcomes. Being completely nonattached is an ideal. As stated earlier, the spiritual or meditative path is not about reaching the ideal, but about being present along the journey. The more nonattached we become, the more peace we can realize.

Some might say, "But if I'm nonattached to what happens in the world, won't I become apathetic? Will I no longer care about the pain and suffering of others if I believe that everything happens for us?" Actually, my experience is the opposite. The more at peace I am within myself, the more I want to help others experience peace. I want to share the inner peace that comes from the knowledge that everything is for us. Peace that comes from having enough food for proper nourishment, a home for security and safety, freedom from abuse and oppression. Interestingly, the degree to which I am nonattached to outcomes is proportionate to my ability to create positive change. When I am attached, I will approach challenges from the level of the problem. When I am nonattached, I will approach challenges from the consciousness of solution.

When we have attachment to any outcome in life, let's say increased health or prosperity, there is always some degree of fear, subtle or not, that what we want to happen won't or what we don't want to happen will. We cannot be at peace when there is attachment and its fuel, fear. When we let go of attachment and therefore are affirming that everything is okay, that we are okay regardless of any outcome, then our energy is freed up, and we have even greater power to create what we might have previously been attached to. The fear puts negative energy into manifesting what we don't want and drains our power to create what we do want. The most powerful consciousness for manifestation of anything is to be clear about what we want and nonattached to how, when, or even if it occurs.

So how do we focus on what we want and be nonattached at the same time? This is obviously a dichotomy. With most, if not all dichotomies of this sort, we can do a "both/and." At the level of Spirit, at the level of Truth, there is no duality, so the both/and brings us into alignment with higher principle.

If it seems like these first three practices have a lot of overlap, it's because they really are different ways of approaching the same goal, which is to be present in each and every moment. It wasn't until I had some experience with these first three that I even knew what it meant to be present in the moment. The more mindful I am, the more I look for the magic in every experience, and the more nonattached I am, the freer I am in each and every moment to experience and appreciate the beauty all around me and even the beauty in what others may label as hideous.

All these practices require an increase in awareness. So how can we increase our awareness in our daily lives? How can we facilitate consistency in these states of being? The following practices can help.

SPIRITUAL CUES

A powerful tool I've employed and taught for more than twenty-five years involves using cues to remain conscious of our intentions to be present, mindful, nonattached, loving, or any other desirable state. There are a couple of different ways to use this tool. One is to create self-directed cues, such as "Every time I walk through a doorway, I will come back to my spiritual intention," or "Every time I look at the time," or "Every time I look at my phone for any reason." For most people these days, that will be a pretty profoundly consistent reminder. If you choose this method, you will likely find it useful to switch to different cues periodically, because we can become immune or insensitive to the cues over time.

The second way to use this tool—my favorite version—is to set some kind of reminder, on your phone, a watch, computer, stove timer (I like the last one, because it causes me to get up and turn it off, so I really have to break the attention to whatever I happen to be focused on). Set the reminder to go off every hour (or whatever time frame works for you), unless you have an appointment, or perhaps you can put your phone on vibrate so the reminder will be activated silently, even in the midst of your meeting. Each time the alarm goes off, notice the quality and content of your thoughts. This will give you a clear picture of the kind of messages you give yourself in various situations. It will create clarity about how you are using your consciousness and to what degree you are being mindful, creative, loving, etc.

As you continue this practice, you will most likely begin to anticipate the alarm and start adjusting your mental outlook before you even hear it. You can take this practice a step further. Upon the sounding of the alarm, or your anticipation of it, in addition to observing your mental process, consciously switch it to one of magical acceptance. Switch it to a state of awe and wonder. Be present in the moment and affirm that you are manifesting your highest potential.

SEVEN-DAY MENTAL DIET

Emmet Fox created this practice and wrote a book about it with the same title, *The Seven-Day Mental Diet*. The practice is to go one entire week without a single negative thought. Okay, we all know this is virtually impossible, especially if you have the occasion to talk to or interact with pretty much anyone. Once again, the point is not to achieve the ideal, but to create awareness on the journey toward the ideal. By embarking on the diet, you will become infinitely more aware of the quality and veracity of your thinking. Once we have the awareness, we empower ourselves to choose differently.

SHIFT AND RELEASE

I developed this method for the purpose of releasing uncomfortable feelings, like outbursts, illness, or unconscious negative patterns, in the moment they occur, rather than suppressing them and having them arise and be expressed in less-desirable ways in the future. This is also a way to avoid the trap of spiritual bypass or suppressing emotions while using techniques to transcend or transmute discomfort.

What normally happens when we get angry, fearful, frustrated, hurt, etc., is that we instantly judge ourselves in a negative way. We all do this to varying degrees. Then the negative spiral downward begins. We feel bad and guilty. Then we rationalize—"Well, I should be angry after what he/she said to me!" Then this inner conversation ensues for minutes, hours, sometimes even days.

What would your life be like if it were 100 percent free of self-judgment?—which is the only kind of judgment there is—because if you judge someone else, you are really just judging a part of yourself you are projecting onto someone else, yes? This simple process is designed to release judgment in the moment and take you back to the spiritual intention you have for your life.

The result is that you will continue to have human responses to challenging situations, but you will only spend seconds or minutes releasing the energy instead of hours or days—which means you will end up with much longer periods of time living in love, creativity, freedom, bliss, and positive expectancy.

Here are the steps to this simple process:

Each morning (at least five days per week), set your intention for the day about what qualities you want to embody, live, and express, such as joy, love, freedom, clarity, bliss. You can do this as part of an already existing meditative practice or simply spend a couple of minutes on it even on days that you may not meditate.

Any time you feel discomfort or tension of any kind that takes you away from your morning intention, let out any emotional energy that needs to be released—pain, fear, anger. If you are in a safe enough place, scream it out! If not, create a cue, like tapping your leg, or simply acknowledge that you are really angry, scared, or hurt. Then without any negative self-judgment for having the reaction—after all, it is a natural human response—do the "shift and release." Place your hand on your heart and say (silently or audibly) "Release and shift" (or if you find a phrase that works better for you, feel free to use that—in fact feel free no matter what). The point is to create as consistent an experience as possible of positivity, joy, freedom, and bliss.

Use the graph on page 128 to chart how many times you were able to shift to a higher frequency of energy using "release/shift" each day (approximately) and the level of frequency of the qualities you were intending to live with that you achieved on a scale of one to ten (ten being highest). By measuring this process, your attention will be drawn to it, which will create more awareness about it and ultimately accelerate your results.

Each morning when you create your intention for the day, include the intention to "raise the frequency" up one degree from where you were the day before. If you were at a level three yesterday, create an intention for it to be at a level four today. If it goes up to six, create an intention the next day for it to be at seven. If it goes down to two, then the following day, intend to raise it back up to three. All this is done without judgment, of course. And if you do judge yourself for falling backward on the scale, don't judge yourself for judging. Give yourself a clean slate each day and in each moment.

THE JOY FACTOR

A practice that I offer in my Joy Factor workshops and a future book with the same title is to wake up in the morning, check your schedule, and ask yourself what will bring you the most joy to do today, and then go and do that. I know—sounds completely impractical, doesn't it? While it may sound impractical, in my experience, also tested with my clients, this may be the most practical thing you can do for your life.

The understanding that has evolved for me over the course of forty-two years of meditation and other spiritual practices is that the secret to a fulfilling and joyful life is living from the inner experience of joy, freedom, and love. When this is accomplished, everything else comes into alignment and life becomes progressively easier and more fulfilling.

How I define joy, by the way, is not "the opposite of sadness"— that's happiness, which is a personal experience. *Joy* for me is a pervasive spiritual quality that can exist even in times of sadness, loss, grief, or anger. *True joy* for me is synonymous with deep connectivity and deep peace. After a massive stroke, my mother had come home to hospice at ninety-three, and we knew she only had a few days left in physical form. This was certainly not a happy time, but it was filled with the pervasive joy I'm referring to. We were connected at a soul level more fully than ever before. We find joy when we give up resistance to our experiences in life, when we immerse ourselves in whatever experience life is offering us and allow ourselves to see the beauty in everything. This is true joy.

If true spiritual joy is not merely the personal experience of happiness, then certainly it is not instant gratification either. The joy of which I write is always lasting or long-term. When asking what will bring me the most joy today or in any decision-making process, I can clarify whether it is long-term joy by asking how I will feel a month or a year from now, having decided to do what brings me joy now. The most powerful and effective way to live from an inner experience of joy is to do what brings us lasting joy on a consistent basis. In fact, the most powerful demonstration of self-love is to do what brings us joy. By asking what will bring you joy and doing it, you are demonstrating to your own psyche that you are deserving of living a life of joy. If you take a day off from work or cancel appointments because you have assessed that going to relax at the beach or mountains or a river will bring you the most lasting joy, you have made a powerful declaration to your own psyche. By continuing to ask what will bring you the most joy and doing it, you will become reacquainted with the joy for which you have chosen these activities.

As human beings, we tend to do what will bring us the most joy, but we forget about the joy for which we are doing them. I might think, "I have to go to this job I don't like," or "I have to raise these teenage kids." By continuing to ask what will bring us the most joy, we refocus on the joy for which we are doing certain activities, what we may have previously called "obligations," "have-tos," or worse, "shoulds."

CONCLUSION

Whatever spiritual practice you employ to expand and integrate your meditation practice, my encouragement to you, my beloved reader, is to do it all with joy and freedom. Give yourself the gift of inner peace, and forgive and accept yourself in each and every moment that you are not experiencing that gift. Know that any and every experience that is inconsistent with how you want to live your life, when embraced and accepted, will offer you incentive and inspiration to choose inner peace, freedom, and love more consistently and fully.

Know that you are in your perfect place on your path toward freedom, and that every step—even the difficult ones—is necessary and perfect. Give yourself a break, my friend. You deserve it. Be gentle with yourself and you will be gentle with others. Love yourself no matter what! I was talking with a client recently about self-love, and the phrasing that came to me was "When I unconditionally love myself just the way I am, I realize I am not myself. I am, in fact, *The Self.* I am, in fact, pure love." And so are you!

Thank you for allowing me to walk with you a bit down your path of unfolding love.

In love and joy!

—PATRICK J. HARBULA

RESOURCES

Training Centers and Organizations

1440 Multiversity in Scotts Valley, California, presents daily classes, weekend discovery adventures, and many other offerings, including Ananda yoga and Kriya yoga.   https://1440.org

Ananda, based on the teachings of Paramahansa Yogananda, has meditation and Kriya yoga training centers in many states in the United States and countries around the world.   www.ananda.org

Breathworks offers Mindfulness-Based Pain Management trainings and teachers' trainings in Manchester and London, England.   www.breathworks-mindfulness.org.uk

Centers for Spiritual Living is an international organization that offers classes in Science of Mind, New Thought metaphysics, and other spiritual subjects, all of which include meditation.   www.cslcs.org

The Chopra Center is located in Carlsbad, California, and offers meditation groups and classes (free introductory) and yoga classes, as well as other services. www.chopra.com

The Christian Meditation Center offers meditation classes, trainings, and retreats in various locations in New Jersey, as well as online tips, a meditation timer, and other services. www.christianmeditation center.org

Esalen is a retreat center in Big Sur, California, offering classes and workshops in many different styles of meditation and yoga as well as other holistic and self-help subjects. www.esalen.org

Findhorn is a world-famous spiritual center in northern Scotland that offers weeklong trainings and residential programs in meditation, sacred dance, yoga, and other holistic subjects. www.findhorn.org

Inner Quest is a metaphysical Christian church in Alpharetta, Georgia, that offers meditation training, energy healing, and other spiritual subjects. www.innerquestchurch.org

Insight Meditation and Retreat Center offers insight (mindfulness and Vipassana) meditation and Buddhist teachings in Redwood City, California. www.insightmeditationcenter.org

The International Society for Krishna Consciousness, also known as the Hare Krishna movement, founded by A. C. Bhaktivedanta Swami Prabhupada, offers free classes, ceremonies, and free vegetarian meals in many locations as well as residential programs. www .iskcon.org and www.krishna.com

The Krishnamurti Foundation of America in Ojai, California, offers meditation training, retreats, and residential programs based on the teachings of Krishnamurti. www.kfa.org

The Maharishi Foundation has Transcendental Meditation training centers all around the world offering programs for meditation training and becoming a trainer. www.tm.org

Omega is a world-famous organization with centers in Rhinebeck, New York; New York, New York; and Costa Rica that offers meditation training and personal and spiritual growth classes and workshops onsite and online. www.eomega.org

OSHO International Meditation Resort is located in Maharashtra, India, and offers many different meditation training options for onsite study.   www.osho.com

Sahaja Yoga Meditation offers classes in various areas of Australia based on the teachings of Shri Mataji Nirmala Devi.   www.freemed itation.com.au

Sai Baba Ashram has three associated communities in India with affordable but not at all fancy accommodations for short or long stays and includes daily meditation and satsang—sitting with a teacher or guru to receive blessings.   www.srisathyasai.org.in

Self-Realization Fellowship was founded by Paramahansa Yogananda and has meditation and Kriya yoga centers in most U.S. states and many countries around the world.   www.yogananda-srf.org

Shinzen Young offers residential meditation retreats and conference-call meditation trainings.   www.shinzen.org

SYDA Foundation offers Siddha yoga training, including meditation, chanting, and yoga based on the teachings of one of the more famous Indian gurus, Swami Muktananda. There are online courses as well as onsite centers and ashrams around the world.   www .siddhayoga.org

Sri Anandamayi Ma was an Indian teacher who was not as well-known in the West as some more famous gurus but was considered a saint by the people of her country, and virtually all the more famous gurus visited her for darshan, or ceremonial worship, because of her high level of spiritual development. There are twenty-four ashrams she founded in India that can be visited for retreat and meditation training.   www.anandamayi.org

Unity Centers is a New Thought Christian organization with centers around the world offering classes in metaphysical study based on the teachings of Myrtle and Charles Fillmore with a strong emphasis on meditation and Eastern philosophy.   www.unity.org

The Vedanta Society, founded by Swami Vivekananda, has centers and live-in facilities around the globe and offers meditation training and classes on the Vedic teachings. All classes are free.   www.vedanta .org

Vipassana Meditation in the tradition of Sayagyi U Ba Khin offers ten-

day Vipassana trainings in many countries around the world.　www
.dhamma.org

Yogaville is a yoga training and retreat facility in Buckingham, Virginia, founded by Swami Satchidananda. It offers meditation training, integral yoga training, and teacher training as well as retreats and residential programs.　www.yogaville.org

You can also find meditation classes and training programs at various Christian churches. Search the net for meditation classes, groups, and training, plus your preferred denomination.

Websites

Dave Potter offers free Mindfulness-Based Stress Reduction classes online, all based on the system developed by Jon Kabat-Zinn at the University of Massachusetts.　www.palousemindfulness.com

The Free Mindfulness Project offers free meditations, videos, discussion forums, poetry, and other mindfulness meditation resources. www.freemindfulness.org/download

Labyrinth Locator offers a database of labyrinths throughout the world. www.labyrinthlocator.com

Meditation Society of Australia offers free online meditation classes, yoga, daily meditations, and other resources. www.meditation.org.au/online.asp

Retreat Finder offers a database of retreats around the world, searchable by meditation style.　www.retreatfinder.com/Directory /Meditation.aspx

Mindful seeks to connect the emergent elements in the mindfulness community and offers simple mindfulness meditation exercises, video conferences, and a bimonthly magazine entitled *Mindful* in both print and digital form.　www.mindful.org

Mindfulness Magazine has an online directory for meditation retreats, classes, and groups.　https://directory.mindful.org

Oprah Winfrey and Deepak Chopra provide a twenty-one-day meditation journey once a year. The twenty-one-day program is free, and each session can be listened to for five days before it is no longer accessible. The program is available for purchase at the end of the journey.   www.chopracentermeditation.com

Quiet Kit offers free, easy meditations and instruction for beginners.
www.quietkit.com

Sahaja Yoga offers a free ten-week online meditation course.
www.onlinemeditation.org

Tracks to Relax offers guided sleep meditations for inducing deep and relaxing sleep.   www.trackstorelax.com

University of Metaphysics, founded by Paul Masters, offers meditations and online metaphysical degrees, including bachelor's, master's, and doctoral.   www.metaphysics.com

World Community for Christian Meditation contains a database of Christian meditation groups, classes, and retreats around the world.
www.wccm-usa.org

Yellow Brick Cinema offers videos with relaxing music and compelling visuals for sleep, study, meditation, and relaxation.
www.youtube.com/channel/UCwobzUc3z-0PrFpoRxNszXQ

Apps

Aura offers new, personalized, three-minute meditations every day.

Headspace is geared toward beginning meditators, and their free trial includes ten exercises that can help you learn about meditation and applying it to daily life.

Insight Timer features more than ten thousand guided meditations from more than a thousand teachers.

The Mindfulness App includes a five-day guided meditation practice, reminders for when it's time to relax, and other offers based on individual meditation habits.

Products

Biofeedback devices: This site offers an unbiased review of four of the most popular mind-calming biofeedback devices: www.chopra.com /articles/the-pros-and-cons-of-4-meditation-gadgets.

Candles: You can find some beautifully colorful candles on Amazon.com by searching for the following: "Himalayan salt tea light candle holder" (beautiful and calming) and "HYMOSY Strong Candles" (colorfully decorated). The following site contains information on using candles for meditation as well as reviews of specific meditation candle products: www.awakeandmindful.com/best-candles -for-meditation.

Crystals: Visit this website for information on crystals for meditation and their specific purposes: www.energymuse.com/blog/meditating -crystals. This site offers information on finding the right crystal for you, crystal meditations, and a large selection for purchase: www.crystalvaults.com.

Cushions, seats, and benches: These two sites have a variety of meditation cushions, seats, and benches: www.gaiam.com/collections /meditation-seating and www.samadhicushions.com. You can also find a fair variety on Amazon.com.

Fountains: You can find lovely fountains on Amazon.com, including this one, which includes three candles and a beautiful tabletop fountain: search for "Alpine WCT202." This one is also very relaxing: search for "Silver Springs Relaxation Fountain." This site offers fountains with Zen Buddhist themes: www.chopa.com/fountains.html.

Incense: You can find just about every kind of incense and olfactory-enhancing product on this site: www.incensewarehouse.com. My favorite stick brand is Satya Sai Baba Nag Champa. I find that there is a higher concentration of the scent in each stick than in other brands.

Light and sound devices: This site offers information and reviews on various brands of light and sound devices as well as a discount to purchase them when clicking through from the site: www.howtolucid.com/best-mind-machines.

Mandalas: The most beautiful and complete array of mandalas I know of all from one artist for viewing and purchase can be found at www .mandalavisions.com. You can find more from a variety of artists to view and purchase at www.art.com. This site has gorgeous wall hanging tapestry mandalas at a very reasonable price:

www.royalfurnish.com. You can also view some beautiful animated mandalas on YouTube, including this one:

www.youtube.com/watch?v=ux7gSKl0Tgw.

Meditation music: In addition to the thousands of guided meditations and meditation music in the apps in the Apps section, a few favorite meditation pieces are: *Pachelbel with Nature's Ocean Sounds* by Gary Sill; *Whalesong* by Tim Wheater; *Music for Healing Mind, Body, and Spirit* by Steven Halpern; *Calm Within: Music for Relaxation of Body and Mind* by Laura Sullivan. All these artists have many more offerings and the list of wonderful New Age and meditation music and artists is virtually endless. You can purchase these selections on Amazon.com as well as other music-specific sites, such as

www.CDbaby.com. You can also listen free to virtually any music you may be interested in by searching for the title and artist on YouTube.com, and with Amazon Prime you can stream the most popular songs. You can also find most songs on the Pandora app or www.pandora.com.

FREQUENCY RAISER

Each day place two dots at the intersection of the lines for the measure and day of the month. The first dot indicates the amount of times you did the release shift process for that day and the second is the rating on a scale of 1 to 10 (10 being the highest), the level that you achieved (averaging the day) of the qualities you intended to live in for that day: joy, bliss, peace, love, freedom, etc. Make copies of this page so you can use them beyond one month.

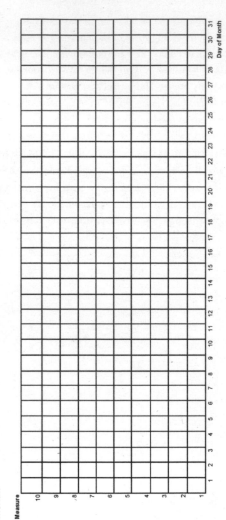

Measure

Day of Month

NOTES

1. WHAT IS MEDITATION?

1. *Merriam-Webster*, s.v. "meditation," www.merriam-webster.com /dictionary/meditation.

2. Ibid.

3. Ibid.

4. *The Free Dictionary*, s.v. "meditation," https://medical-dictionary .thefreedictionary.com/meditation.

2. BENEFITS OF MEDITATION

1. Helen Lavretsky et al., "A Randomized Controlled Trial of Kundalini Yoga in Mild Cognitive Impairment," *International Psychogeriatrics* 29, no. 4 (April 2017): 557–567, https://doi.org/10.1017 /S1041610216002155.

2. *World Disease Weekly* Editors, "Neuroscience; Meditation Appears to Be Associated with Structural Changes in the Brain," *World Disease Weekly; Atlanta* 29 (November 2005): 1237.

3. Fadel Zeidan et al., "Mindfulness Meditation-Based Pain Relief Employs Different Neural Mechanisms than Placebo and Sham Mindfulness Meditation-Induced Analgesia," *Journal of Neuroscience* 35, no. 46 (November 18, 2015): 15307–15325, https://doi.org/10.1523/JNEUROSCI.2542-15.2015.

4. Richard J. Davidson et al., "Alterations in Brain and Immune Function Produced by Mindfulness Meditation," *Psychosomatic Medicine* 65, no. 4 (July 2003): 564–570, DOI: 10.1097/01.PSY.0000077505.67574.E3.

5. S. Annells et al., "Meditate Don't Medicate: How Medical Imaging Evidence Supports the Role of Meditation in the Treatment of Depression," *Radiography* 22, no. 1 (February 2016): e54–e58, https://doi.org/10.1016/j.radi.2015.08.002.

6. Yogesh Singh et al., "Immediate and Long-Term Effects of Meditation on Acute Stress Reactivity, Cognitive Functions, and Intelligence," *Alternative Therapies in Health and Medicine* 18, no. 6 (November/December 2012): 46–53, https://pdfs.semanticscholar.org/dd01/c564fcfb2a1d86b7b6bfa0eaf4a42fdd6cdd.pdf.

7. University of Pennsylvania, "Meditate to Concentrate," *ScienceDaily* 26 (June 2007), www.sciencedaily.com/releases/2007/06/070625193240.htm.

8. Jon Kabat-Zinn et al., "Effectiveness of a Meditation-Based Stress Reduction Program in the Treatment of Anxiety Disorders," *The American Journal of Psychiatry* 149, no. 7 (July 1992): 936–43. DOI: 10.1176/ajp.149.7.936.

9. Patrick Harbula, "The Many Roads Home," *Meditation Magazine* 3, no. 3 (Summer 1988).

10. Reprinted with permission from Daniel Nahmod, "One Power." Words and Music by Daniel Nahmod, © Nahmod Music Co. (ASCAP).

11. Patrick Harbula, "Pir Vilayat Inayat Khan," *Meditation Magazine* 2, no. 2 (Spring 1987).

3. GETTING STARTED

1. Patrick Harbula, *The Magic of the Soul: Applying Spiritual Power to Daily Living* (Thousand OaksCA: Peak Publications, 2003).

4. MEDITATION PRACTICE

1. Harbula, *The Magic of the Soul*. Modified from "Zen Tennis Exercise," 156.

2. Harbula, *The Magic of the Soul*. Modified from "The Fires of My Mind," 156.

3. Harbula, *The Magic of the Soul*. Modified from "Exercise for Stilling the Mind," 122.

4. Harbula, *The Magic of the Soul*. Modified from "Sun Meditation," 199.

5. Modified from "The Great Invocation," Lucis Trust, www.lucistrust.org/the_great_invocation.

5. SUPPORTING SPIRITUAL PRACTICES

1. Michael Jordan, edited by Mark Vancil, *For the Love of the Game: My Story* (New York: Crown Publishers, 2008), 64.

2. Pam Grout, *E³: Nine More Energy Experiments that Prove Manifesting Magic and Miracles Is Your Full-Time Gig* (Carlsbad, CA: Hay House, 2014), 122.

3. Ibid, 120.

INDEX

About the Author

Christina Neferis

PATRICK J. HARBULA is the founder of the Living Purpose Institute and has been a leader and teacher in the human potential movement, meditation trainer, and life coach for over thirty years. He is the author of *The Magic of the Soul: Applying Spiritual Power to Daily Living.* Patrick continues to reach hundreds of thousands with his empowering message of living in peace, joy, and love. He appears regularly on radio and TV around the US and in Canada including Dateline, ABC, NBC, and UPN news.